God Bless,
Michelle

Thriving in Chaos

MICHELLE MALLOY

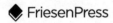 FriesenPress

One Printers Way
Altona, MB R0G 0B0
Canada

www.friesenpress.com

Edited by Crystal Picard
Cover design by Crystal Picard

Self-Published by Michelle Malloy Counselling
Halifax, Nova Scotia
Canada B3L 2V3
www.peddlinghope.com

For information about special discounts for bulk purchases, please contact Special Sales at counselling@michellemalloy.ca

ISBN
978-1-03-916886-2 (Hardcover)
978-1-03-916885-5 (Paperback)
978-1-03-916887-9 (eBook)

1. SELF-HELP, PERSONAL GROWTH

Distributed to the trade by The Ingram Book Company

This book is dedicated to Dan, MacGregor & Brogan –
I could only be me because of each one of you.
I love you all beyond measure.

DISCLAIMER

All stories in this book are fictitious unless otherwise indicated. Any resemblance to actual persons, living or dead, is purely coincidental.

Although the author is a Registered Counselling Therapist and educated in the areas of trauma and grief recovery, this publication is designed to provide information only and is not a substitution for specific, individual therapy. Any errors, inaccuracies, omissions, or any other inconsistencies herein are not the responsibility of either the publisher or the author.

This publication is meant as a source of information for the reader. It is not meant to replace direct expert assistance. If such level of assistance is required, the sources of a competent professional should be sought.

TABLE OF CONTENTS

INTRODUCTION
Thriving IN CHAOS

In the DreamWorks animated film Shrek, a conversation between Shrek and Donkey comes to my mind when I think about trauma and healing. In an effort to appear multi-dimensional, Shrek tells his companion that ogres are like onions—they have many layers. Donkey counters that, unlike onions, cakes and parfaits have layers too, and everyone loves them! There are lots of things in life that have layers, your story is among them. Life is complex, often complicated, and can be thought of as chapters in your story. Like ogres, people are multi-dimensional, which adds to the complexity.

When given the options for a book cover, I chose the version that looks like an oil painting. It made for the perfect analogy because oil paintings are created in layers. They begin as blobs of colour and become a beautiful masterpiece. As a kid, my family was enchanted with Bob Ross' *The Joy Of Painting*. Each week we would watch as he added layer upon layer, slowly bringing the final landscape into view. He always had a plan for how he wanted things to go, but he could go-with-the-flow when accidents happened. Those accidents became a happy little bird or an additional tree. It never stopped his work.

As I researched a little more about how to work with oil paints, I found "7 oil painting techniques that every artist should know", an article by Gareth Evans where he lays out the three rules of oil painting:

- Fat over lean

- Thick over thin

- Slow-drying over fast-drying

"Each layer of paint should be progressively more flexible and thicker and slow-drying than the one below it. It stops each layer from cracking." This explanation for oil painting seemed to make the analogy even clearer to me. I began to think of fat and thick like our circumstances and situations in life while lean and thin are more like our thoughts and emotions. So often we get stuck in thought-loops or feelings of overwhelm and can lose our focus on the bigger picture. I find the idea of zooming out to take in the whole canvas appealing. Slow over fast appeals to me as well. In a world so focused on being busy, the idea that slow is better feels so contrary, and perhaps impossible. Yet, the faster we move the greater chance we have of cracking. That sounds about right.

As values guide our lives, techniques guide an artist as they bring their painting to completion. Our character, values and principles are like the under-coat of paint, setting the foundation of our lives. It's important to set things up right when you're learning to thrive in chaos. Steps in painting with oil seem to fit for comparison:

Gather your materials: these can be the people or things in your environment that will allow healing and growth. We need to be aware of what those are specifically as we venture into this book to create a vision for our lives.

Set up a safe work space: safety is key. Our instinct is for safety and our nervous system will not cooperate if it is not in a state of safety. It will prepare for a fight/flight response and conserve energy from all other parts of our life in preparation for danger.

Prime your canvas: this work is foundational. Generational trauma, which we explore in chapter 7, is a way of understanding what is on the canvas already. None of us start life with a clean slate. We are all born into family systems with assumptions and biases in the ways of being in the world that will be passed on to us as we grow up. Priming is uncovering what is on the canvas already and beginning from there.

Outline your painting: having a plan for where you'd like to end up begins with an idea that can be fleshed out as you go. It is not necessarily what the painting will look like in the end, but it is a guide for how you'd like it to look in the end. Perhaps it follows the outline and you can recognize where you started. Perhaps the picture looks completely different because you've decided to go in a different direction. (There may even be some happy little birds or trees you've created from a mess along the way.)

Layer your paint: we already know our canvas is not blank. We cannot "start from scratch" as we enter into this journey together. All of us come with many parts of the story already told—the paint already on the canvas. Instead, we will explore what's on there and figure out how to work from that point. We may have different colours or textures, but the technique will be the same for all of us embarking on this journey together.

Wipe off excess: although this is more about the brushes than the painting, I thought it was a good thing to keep in mind. Cleaning your tools as you go gets rid of the build-up, which can interfere with what you want to do next. Old patterns in our life that we created to protect us in the moment may no longer serve us in our current situation. Recognizing them and understanding where they came from is important, but then we need to clean them off. It's excess that will interfere with what we are trying to create. We will explore that idea a little more in chapter four on letting go.

Through the chapters, we will explore and create our stories in the way an artist skilled in oil painting would: contrasting between light and dark aspects (Chiaroscuro) and texturing as we go (Scumbling), understanding and firming up our foundation as you would in Underpainting where you sketch a thin layer on the canvas of life, or outline the story in that analogy. We live our lives adding layers that make it into a multi-faceted creation, what oil painters call Glazing.

This book will aim to take a similar approach to understanding our selves and our lives in an effort to build upon what is there already and then adding to those layers as we go. The first part of the book (chapters 1-3) we start at the beginning. We'll explore our collective yearning for change, which is why you may have picked up this book and is certainly why I wrote it. We will focus on the elements of understanding different aspects and parts of our self that will expand our self-awareness and then work through how to hold space for what we discover.

The second part of the book (chapters 4-6) will tackle some of the difficult stuff that can make life more complicated and perhaps messier than we imagined it should be. Once we bring various elements into awareness, there may be some parts of our story that need healing. Situations and events through our lives may have left traumatic wounds; so, we will take a deeper dive there to determine what needs to be let go so we can move more fully into an atmosphere of acceptance and love.

Lastly, we will spend some time (chapters 7-9) considering how to bring the picture more clearly into focus and adding some finishing touches. This will include the parts of our self or our story that need to be changed so we can sketch our goals for the future and begin living our lives with intention and purpose. Each part of this book is meant to layer upon the part that came before it, bringing the story more clearly into focus. In order to do that, I have included reflective questions and exercises, as well as other stories that illustrate the points I'm trying to make. As Otto von Bismarck tells us, "Only a fool learns from his own mistakes. The wise man learns from the mistakes of others." The same can be said for struggles. Although they feel very individual, many of us have shared experiences from which we can learn, so I will use them as a point of connection.

My own story of loss and trauma is included because it is those chapters of my life journey that have become the foundation of my life today. The client stories I write about are actually several people's stories woven together. The stories and the insights that came to each individual client are all real, but the people I've included are not. The story is meant to make the point but not disclose any personal information or distinguishing features. If someone in the book sounds familiar, it may be that you know someone who has gone through something similar. I wanted to include stories that are common struggles, whose insights may be relevant to similar situations in our own lives. Being social creatures, we learn from one another.

My hope in writing this book is that you see yourself in the struggles as we work through the chapters and that you find your own insights that can help you heal your wounds, or at least begin the process. I have worked to arm you with some techniques for healing and made space for you to dream a little and set your path. In reflecting on the past, we can learn lessons from the experiences we have had. Rather than carrying all the hurt and pain, the lesson we carry can be like something big that folds into something compact and light for a long journey. Focusing on the future is meant to forge a destination that becomes familiar so that we recognize it when it comes into view.

Learning what it means to live in the present, however, is a key element I have woven through the whole book. Being mindful and present is knowing that the journey itself is the best part of travelling to your destination. I want to generate enthusiasm for the process of becoming. No one wants to get to the end of their life having made good time but missing all the sights along the way. Being present means being aware. Awareness expands into action to help you move, heal and grow, and help others do the same.

The book is a creation, like an oil painting. We learn and layer, blend and integrate. Our life is also a creation. Goals and aspirations are part of that creation but they're not the only thing. Learning to live mindfully in the moment is the key to thriving in a chaotic environment. We may not be able to control all the elements around us, but in a constantly changing world, we can find ways to heal and grow and thrive regardless. My hope is that the connections you make as you read will help the picture of your life's journey come clearly into view.

CHAPTER ONE

YEARNING FOR *Change*

How to take stock before you take the next step

---

*"What if the question is not why am I so infrequently
the person I really want to be, but why do I so infrequently
want to be the person I really am?"*

Oriah Mountain Dreamer

"Who am I?" is a big question—one of the most powerful questions there is. We all tend to ask it at some point in our lives. I know I am more than my labels: a woman, a wife, a mom, a twin, a therapist. The question is usually who am I beyond my gender, nationality, or ethnicity; beyond my job, beyond my roles. "Who am I *really*?" The other big question most of us are grappling with is, "Why am I here?" These questions are so big they can stop us in our tracks. The challenge is that these questions have no definitive answer. They can be circular, which means they show up at different ages and stages of life. Asking these big questions gives us opportunities for reflection and contemplation. They can provide a deeper level of insight. We can go a little further each time: "Who am I underneath the ego?" or "Who am I deep in my soul?" These are the questions that guide us towards meaning. Looking for the *right* answer, however, can ultimately hold us back from doing meaningful, reflective work.

In addition to these internal identity questions, we take our questioning to an external level by asking, "What is my purpose?" The question implies there is a reason why I am here—I *am meant to do something.* It is similar to "Why am I here?" but it takes us outside ourselves. These questions are ones of service taking the insights we get from asking, "Who am I?" to a practical level. Asking, "How can I serve?" shifts the focus because it brings in the external world. For example, if I ask "Who am I?" and find that I care deeply about social justice issues, I can spend a lot of time trying to figure out why. But to what end? Maybe I care about social justice issues because of my own experience of being a victim of injustice. Acknowledging the fact that I care, for whatever reason, is internal. Asking, "How can I serve?" takes me outside myself towards action.

Asking questions for the sake of getting answers can be frustrating, especially when there are no definitive answers but only possibilities. Asking for the sake of curiosity can be a valuable process, however. If we are curious about who we are, we may be surprised by what we find. Once we begin to engage with these questions—"Who am I?" and "How can I serve?"—in an effort to more fully understand our self, we transform. It is an opportunity to challenge old patterns. It helps us identify stories in our past we have outgrown, stories with labels that no longer serve us. It is about living from the point of view of intention.

Asking questions and being curious about who we are and our purpose in life can also bring about compassion for ourself. It is a way to honour any suffering we may have experienced so that we can find meaning, which powers us forward. Our power fuels us; gives us the energy to change and grow. It puts us in the driver's seat, so we act in our life rather than react to our circumstances. The only thing we can truly do with our lives is give them away. Whether it is giving away love, hope, forgiveness, or compassion, we must start with our self. By giving these things to our self, a deeper understanding of who we are emerges and connects us to our soul, our core. It is at our core where spirit lifts us out of self and connects us in a very meaningful way to the world around us.

Thriving in a world of chaos begins with contemplating these bigger life questions. I genuinely believe that the human spirit is about seeking.

It is less about getting to the end and more about the process of living. This way of being in the world is different from aligning with a world that encourages us to *constantly strive* for more. There is nothing inherently wrong with striving towards a goal. But, if that is all we do, we miss the experience of living life. How often do you stop to enjoy the journey towards the goal you were striving for? Regardless of what it might be—a degree, partner, house, promotion—you likely set another goal to strive towards as soon as the achievement of the previous one has been met.

Similarly, the endless pursuit of self-improvement can leave us feeling "less than". This book will help you set goals for your future, but not without examining how you got to where you are in the first place. The constant striving for improvement keeps us in a never-ending pursuit of that magic solution. Western culture teaches us that being happy is the ultimate goal of life. Happy is a great emotion! However, it's too fleeting to be a life goal.

Tidying Up expert Marie Kondo asks us to consider our physical belongings by asking, "Do I want to bring this with me into my future?" We must ask the same question about our emotional lives. Some ways of being in the world are generational, leading us to perpetuate the cycle without ever considering if these patterns fit us personally. We need to take time periodically to sort through our stories, look for the chapters that no longer serve us, and heal the things that are barriers to living in joy.

Living in a constant state of striving can leave us perpetually chasing life instead of enjoying it. We may always feel as if we are behind in some way. The goal here is self-awareness, which is an expansion of self. By understanding who we are in more detail and from different vantage points, we grow. It's inevitable. I long for a life of contentment, fulfillment, meaning and purpose. If you do too, then I invite you to take this journey of self-reflection with me.

MYTH OF SISYPHUS

In Greek mythology, Sisyphus was a king who Hades punished for trying to cheat death. Each morning, Sisyphus was required to roll a giant boulder up a hill only to have it roll back down at the end of the day. For eternity! Life can often feel like that. This weight—*isn't it the weight I lost last* year? This debt—*haven't I paid this off already?* This habit—*should I even try again to change it?* It seems we do these things over and over. We set goals each new year, intending to make long-lasting change and then, like Sisyphus, we feel doomed to set and reset these goals forever.

Some philosophers believe that Sisyphus is simply a representation of the sun. It rises and then sets each day. Others use a similar analogy but say it is the ebb and flow of the tides or the inhale and exhale of the breath. Sisyphus could be the struggle of man—a vain daily struggle that leads to nowhere. Albert Camus believed the myth of Sisyphus is man's struggle to reach high heights to fill our hearts. If that is true, that our hearts are filled in the process of living our lives, then there must be meaning in the process.

This is where meaning plays an important part in motivation to keep rolling that stone uphill. Ask yourself: "What significance do my goals have in relation to the person I want to be or the life I want to live?" Often, we will set our goals or make resolutions because of some ideal or societal pressure to be a certain weight, have a certain income level, or live a particular lifestyle. This pressure can push us to examine our life only through an external lens. But what about our internal lives? If you set intentions or goals, ask yourself: "Why is this important to me?" Do it several times to really get down deep into why it is meaningful. You may find that it is not that important at all. The ultimate question then becomes:

WHO DO I WANT TO BE?

The answer to that question is often found in our stories. Past experiences and struggles can help us define our lives. Everything that has ever happened has brought us to this point in time. In books, the prologue provides all the necessary information for the story to begin. It is an opportunity to meet characters where they are at that specific moment in time. The thing I love best about a prologue is that it does not determine the story; it simply informs it. Everything that has happened up until now is merely the background. It provides context. As a reader, we don't limit the story based on the prologue. We keep reading. Whether the character is real or fictional, we know there is more to the story.

Your story is the same. Yet, how often do we limit what *can* happen based on what has *already* happened. What if instead, we saw everything that has happened to date as a prologue to new possibilities. Beyond the prologue is the whole story. There are many more pages to explore. In fact, if you skip to the end, there is an epilogue. Curiosity keeps us reading. We want to know how the character gets from the prologue to the epilogue. The difference between a book and our lives is that the author of a book often writes the epilogue first. In the case of a biography, the story is reflective.

What if you wrote the epilogue of your life today? How different might your life be if you had a vision for how it all turns out? How much influence would that yield in how your story plays out? Think about the amount of influence you would have in your life if you wrote your legacy first. By writing how you want the story to end, you set the path of intention. Each day would be living intentionally to bring that dream into existence. When following along with a character in a book, we know there will be obstacles to overcome. By having written the ending first, we have the opportunity to look at these challenges with curiosity: "How will I conquer this one?"

We all want the struggle in our lives to be meaningful. It is only in looking backwards that we can see the meaning we have made from our life's challenges. In retrospect, we see how challenges and our reactions to them have influenced our life story. It is often hard to find the meaning in the middle of a challenge. If we think from the end (epilogue) and consider everything that has gotten us to the here and now (prologue) as only part of the story, it empowers us to find and live our life's purpose in the present. It encourages us towards a life lived in curiosity and adventure. It takes us from passively wondering what happens next to taking up a pen and writing.

We all have a story inside us waiting to be told. It is up to each of us to claim its authorship. This book is a beginning: looking at our story, putting down the things that make pushing the boulder uphill harder, and setting an intention for living an inspired life. Striving to achieve something in our lives is part of living intentionally, but it is future-focused. Thriving means knowing that rolling the boulder is part of the process and then making it a meaningful part.

EXPLORING OUR LANGUAGE

Exploring our story, our narrative, is a way of looking at our lives and seeing how it aligns with our core values. In therapy, I use externalization as a tool for seeing a problem or belief as just that: a problem or a belief. A challenge in life is not the whole story. Your response to it may come from a lot of different places. It really depends on the environment you grew up in. Language is the key to finding perspective around life's challenges and our own sense of self. For example, when a person feels depressed, they often say, "I am depressed." It is the "I am" that is so key in that statement. We don't say, "I am cancer." We say, "I have cancer." When we say "I am" we can over-identify with that part of our story. Depression, anxiety, feelings of loss may be the dominating theme at that time, but it is only one part of our whole life story.

Describing our thoughts or feelings as something external, we can stay centered, strong, and in control; we are always more than just our thoughts and feelings. Seeing them as separate from us means we can cultivate a relationship with them. There are two parts to the experience of *self*. One part is observing (that is, the subjective "I") and the other is being observed (that is, the objective "me or mine"). Depression then can be something we experience: "my depression". When it is external (or objective), it means we can choose to sit with it and ask why it has come (or come back). What is it trying to tell us about our life? This is a way of interacting with the thoughts or feelings rather than being overtaken by it. If we deny, resist, ignore; we are at risk for these thoughts and feelings to come rushing in, often overwhelming us and leaving us feeling helpless. They require so much more attention then.

The challenge is to sit with the feelings without being afraid of them or trying to rescue ourselves from them. Suffering is one of the four truths of life, according to the Buddha. Jesus also teaches on suffering. Our current culture pushes *against* this idea. We welcome the thoughts and feelings we have labeled "positive" but want to avoid those we have labeled "negative." Labelling is a form of judgment. We judge the thoughts and feelings called positive as *good* and those called negative as *bad*. No one in their right mind wants to experience bad things. Too many thoughts and feelings labeled negative or bad begin to alter the way we think about ourselves and our lives. Rather than seeing the thoughts or feelings as external—something we experience—we now see them as character flaws. We do not want to sit and explore any of those things. We want to push them out as quickly as possible and get back to feeling good.

We cannot bear to experience suffering. When we see it in other people, we may feel compelled to rescue them from their pain. Trungpa Rinpoche, a Tibetan Buddhist meditation master and founder of Shambhala, calls that "idiot compassion"—our tendency to give people what they want because we cannot bear their suffering. We need to remember that the same goes for our self. When there is suffering, that situation or feeling seems to take over our life. Everything else may seem intangible or out of control. We will explore this more deeply in subsequent chapters, but for now, consider this—we can lose our sense of self when we over-identify with the world around us. It is easy to get sucked into the story—the thoughts, feelings, events and circumstances—and lose our perspective. When that happens, we may feel like a character in our story at the mercy of life's next plot twist.

We can, however, choose to experience life as it passes through us. Imagine for a moment that the feeling of sadness washes over you. You are not the sadness, you allow yourself to *experience* the sadness. Perhaps there is a situation that warrants sadness, perhaps not. Rather than getting sidetracked with trying to figure out where it came from or deciding if it is reasonable for you to be feeling sad, you simply allow it. You witness it. You are the person (the conscious self) who is witnessing the experience of sadness. Once you have become aware that you are not the feeling, but rather, you are witnessing and experiencing the feeling; it is much easier to validate it and let it go.

This process of witnessing and validating thoughts and feelings may feel reasonable if they flicker in and out of our lives. But, what do you do when they decide to settle in? Even in longer periods of suffering, you can lean in and take time to consider who you are and who you want to be. If we can be still and have compassion for our self in the experience, then there can be meaning and direction. Light follows darkness. You decide who you are and who you want to be. You write your own story, even when life is difficult and challenging you to your core. I feel hopeful that we can find meaning in just about anything that happens in life regardless of circumstances. We can use that meaning perspective to help us grow and change. It does not mean the situation is any less painful when we are going through it. It does mean that we can use what we have learned through that struggle. We can be fortified by it and stand strong—born again into the life we are destined to live.

ANCHORING IN OUR VALUES

Values anchor us in who we are and can help us withstand the difficult times in life. If you aspire to a particular way of life, whether it is picking up something new or putting down an old habit, think about how it relates to your sense of self. Once you find the meaning in it—the *why* behind your aspiration—it's easier to find the motivation to make a change. Motivation is the fuel for doing the things we do. It is the thing that will get you out of bed in the morning. The thing that keeps you from eating the comfort food when the desire for comfort threatens to overwhelm you. The thing that keeps you saving your money when that perfect product shows up in your newsfeed screaming, "Buy me!" It is alignment with your values that anchors you to your long-term goals and dreams.

Our values provide the stability we need to stretch and grow. Think of a tree—its roots reach deep into the earth so the tree itself does not blow over in a storm. The deeper the roots, the sturdier the tree. Deep roots and a sturdy trunk (core) allow the branches to reach high and to bloom periodically. A healthy environment for a tree has sunlight, water, and rich soil. We need the wind to strengthen the bark. The tree is part of an ecosystem of animals, birds, insects. Everything contributes to the health and well-being of the tree itself. We live in a similar ecosystem. Each year, we emerge from a season of rest and reflection—Winter into Spring—a chance to plant new seeds. But, we must also rake the dead leaves to create room for new growth. Such is the balance of nature.

Trees grow in the ecosystem they are born into. So do we. We call our ecosystem "family". Every family system has history, patterns, biases and beliefs. Some systems support us so we thrive right out of the gate, while others require us to struggle and push through the constraints. Both nature and family systems can produce strong trees. But in some cases, the systems need extra attention and care. Think about old patterns or biases that may not fit with the values that are important to you as old, dead roots that are limiting the tree's growth. Establishing an environment for optimal healing and health begins with your own personal values.

Your values are your roots: the thing that grounds you, nurtures you, motivates you towards continual growth. Just as an acorn becomes an oak tree, we are destined to become who we are meant to become. It is in our DNA. While we may have values that are passed on generationally, each of us must decide for ourselves what belongs to us individually. Values must be chosen freely after thoughtful contemplation. When we could have chosen from a number of options, we chose the things that align with who we are and who we want to be in the world rather than simply taking on the values passed down through generations.

Values strengthen our sense of self. When presented with a situation in life, it is easier to decide if we can answer yes or no by asking, "Does this align with my values?" When our values become part of who we are, they show up in our everyday actions. We must be who we are meant to be.

- What do you consider the elements of a healthy environment in your life?

- What do you consider the conditions you need in your life to grow to your fullest potential?

- What do you consider the outside influences in your life?

- Are there patterns that limit your growth?

MAKING DECISIONS

Go to school or travel? Take the job or start a business? Have kids or have money? (The last one is a joke...sort of.) Have you ever found yourself feeling paralyzed trying to make a decision? It is usually fear of making a mistake that keeps us feeling stuck. The wrong choice can mean disadvantage or disappointment. When faced with a choice, we all want to make the best decision possible. The challenge is that there is no *correct* answer. There is only choice. You make the best decision for you at the time, with the information you have at hand. Or maybe there is more to it than that.

John's Story

John was in the process of making a tough decision about his career. His company was in the midst of downsizing and had offered some managers a buyout. John was one of those managers. He agonized about making the wrong decision. For John, everything seemed to come down to one of two options. Either: stay on the corporate fast track with the regular salary increases and all the recognition and continue his life in the big city. Or: take a buyout and open a small business in his hometown where his kids could be closer to their grandparents. Each option came with risks.

Choosing the first option meant John was taking a chance that he would be downsized at some later stage and may not receive the same financial benefit being offered, but there was also a chance he would keep the corporate lifestyle—big salary, social gatherings, living in the city, travelling abroad. Choosing the second option meant John would be starting over—potentially becoming a statistic should his business fail. Plus, he worried about what people would say about him without the corporate position. It was such a big part of his identity. However, he would be back home where his kids could run in the park and walk home from school.

Should he gamble and stay or take the package and leave? No matter how we feel about making a change, transition comes with some loss. You always leave something behind. John and I talked about this upcoming transition from the perspective of loss. How was loss experienced in his family? John was only 8 years old when his family moved to the town he now calls home. At the time, it came with a lot of excitement. His dad had gotten a job, which was a huge relief. He would have his own room for the first time in his young life. There was a baseball team in the community where he could play. However, John was distraught about leaving his best friend, Ethan. They had been inseparable from the day they met at Miss Shirley's Preschool.

Our families are the first social group to which we belong. Our upbringing has a major impact on how we see ourselves, others and the world. It anchors us and becomes our "normal". It is the basis for how we judge everything. Our primary need is to have our physiological and biological needs met, so we may not want to rock the boat if we find ourselves questioning things within our family of origin. We have a fundamental need to be safe and belong, so it can feel dangerous to go against the norm and unearth the foundation. Our parents and caregivers are also products of their environments. The family system they create probably looks a lot like the one they grew up in. We continue to do things or say things that our parents did or said. Ever speak to your kids and hear your mother?

The problem comes when there is a dilemma—when our personal thoughts or values seem to conflict with our family of origin. If we think differently, we may feel so insecure that we question ourselves and our decisions. What if we are wrong? Until someone within the system has the courage to question the system itself; nothing will change.

CHANGING THE STORY

In working through his history, John was able to identify key messages that were part of his family. Messages that seemed to be obstacles to clearly thinking through his current situation. For example, job stability was considered to be the cornerstone of a family. And, it was a dad's responsibility to make sure the family was financially secure. John's grandfather had grown up in the Depression Era, so it was easy to see where these ideas of stability had come from.

There was also a message underlying any struggle in his family that you should always look on the bright side. Wanting their children to have a worry-free upbringing, John's parents were determined to focus on the bright side of every situation, just as their parents had done. What was meant to be loving and protective ended up making John feel terrible. He grieved for his friend after he moved but felt he could not talk about it. He had learned early that grief was not something discussed in his home.

As John objectively explored some of these foundational messages, it was much easier for him to be honest about what *he* really wanted. For him, the most important thing was his immediate family and that they all had a voice in the process. Talking it through with his wife and children was new for John. But, he could empathize with his boys when they talked about leaving their school and friends. In the end, John decided that the best thing to do financially was to take the package and leave his company. His family then decided a new start in a smaller town was a better fit for them than staying in the big city. Finally, John worked through what he would say to people about his decision and where he would get support in the transition.

Have you ever wondered why you do the things you do or think the things you think? We all become part of the story we are born into. The good news is we can pick up the pen at any time and change the narrative if we want. It may not be easy, but by writing our own story we are writing chapters for the next generation. The changes we make in our life influence the family of origin stories of our children and grandchildren.

ASSESSING READINESS FOR CHANGE

One thing that may help you move forward when you're stuck is understanding where you are before taking a step. Once you have determined what values are grounding you, you may find that you want to make changes in your life so your environment aligns with those values.

Stage 1: Precontemplation

This is where you may not even realize you have something that needs changing. Alternatively, you know you need to do something *someday* because you recognize that change is good for you long-term. You can see the benefits, but you may not feel quite ready. Perhaps your confidence in your ability to change is low. You think, "I've tried that before. It doesn't stick."

These old thought patterns and family stories are the things that can keep you stuck; however, ignoring a problem does not make it go away. If you find yourself in the precontemplation stage of change, take a moment to consider where your life is going. You may need to analyze who you are and what you want and then assess the risks of continuing to move forward in life as it is currently structured. Reading this book may help you make that assessment. If you are ready to thrive in life by following your own path, you may be ready to contemplate a change.

Stage 2: Contemplation

Thinking about making a change is the first tangible step. That may be all you are doing at this point, but making a decision is an important place to start. You can get off to a strong start if you feel excited about making a change in your life. You may be motivated by something or someone encouraging you. You may have hit that "last straw" moment where you are sick and tired of being sick and tired. Excitement about making a shift is what propels you forward. Of course, there is also the danger that you will stay stuck or give up hope entirely if you lack a sense of urgency. "I'll start on Monday" (after the holidays, or in the new year) is the kiss of death.

Timing is important. If you do not feel the time is right or that you are equipped to make a change, you may not make the move to the next stage. Be sure the reason you want to change is not fear-based but rather grounded in your personal values. If you feel conflicted or ambivalent, take time to weigh the pros and cons of changing and of not changing. Tim Ferris calls this fear-setting. It's like goal-setting, but it considers the risk of *not changing* by looking at what you are *not achieving* by staying in the same place. Even if you are ready to make a change, consider the possible barriers that may be in your way. Identifying these barriers to change and success is part of the preparation for the journey.

Stage 3: Preparation

You are ready to go! You are going to *do it* this time! You may be taking small steps to get ready—telling your friends and family about your new commitment and thinking about a start date. What may hold you back is skipping the preparation stage altogether and jumping right into action. Preparation is the stage where you need to gather the skills and knowledge for success. Do you have what you need to start strong? Ask for help or support at this stage to make sure you can be successful long-term. Be specific about what you are trying to achieve. It should be measurable so you can see the change. You may begin experimenting with small changes first. There is a lot of excitement in the preparation stage, so be sure to have some affirmations and encouraging statements to keep you on track when willpower wains. It is the decisions for success made at this stage that will push you through when your motivation runs out. Ready. Set. Go!

Stage 4: Action

You're *doing it!* You have prioritized this in your life, and now you are moving. The most important thing is to take small steps each day towards change. It is not quite a habit yet, so you need to be prepared for setbacks and obstacles. It can take a little while for your brain to develop a new way of thinking. How you talk to yourself at this stage can help. I can usually get in an extra push-up or two if I count out loud or say to myself, as T. Harv Eker says, "How you do anything is how you do everything." That voice in my head is like my own personal performance coach. The more I tell myself that, the easier it is for me to complete my routine.

You have to do something long enough for it to become part of the *new you*. People who make a lifestyle change are more likely to be successful than those going on a diet, for example. One is long-term, the other is time-specific. The thing that may get in the way of success at this stage is our resistance to change. We get comfortable in our habits and may be reluctant to change them, even if we really want to change. It may feel like breaking in a new pair of slippers when your old ones were the best slippers ever.

Some people like you better or are more comfortable with the old you. Ever try ordering a salad when everyone else is getting wings? It can feel weird for everyone at the table. "Just this once" or "give yourself a treat" or "everything in moderation" are comments meant to make the person *saying* them feel better. If it was about you, they would be more supportive of your choice with an encouraging word or by saying nothing at all. Social support is essential in this phase, and it may sabotage your efforts if you do not get it.

Another risk is that we want to start seeing results right away. Remember: progress is what you want to measure but outcomes may be out of your control. I can only control that I got myself to the gym, not whether or not I can do 50 push-ups in a row quite yet. (Disclaimer: as of this writing, I cannot do 50 push-ups in a row.) Reward yourself for showing up and taking action. The results will come. I promise.

Stage 5: Maintenance

This is where the habit has been forged. You have been in action for a little while, and the change is now part of your routine. It is not something you have to think about as much. There may be new groups of people engaging in your new lifestyle, encouraging you to show up and have a positive attitude. The most important part of keeping this new behaviour going is knowing there may be situations or people that trigger you to relapse into your old ways.

You may get bored or hit a plateau or maybe a big life event takes you off track. If you plan for it, it is easier to get back on track; otherwise, you may get stuck feeling frustrated or disappointed with yourself. Maintenance is about continually re-committing to thriving in life. There will be storms. Life events may take the legs from under us, but if we see the changes in our life as sustaining us, it is harder to fall back into old patterns and habits that did not work. These changes are foundational. Our new way of being in the world, the unique perspective we have about our life and suffering, helps us weather the storm.

We are not able to control our external circumstances all the time. What we *can* control is the plan for relapse. Planning for it means we are less likely to fall down the rabbit hole of guilt, anger, disappointment, or hopelessness. Maintenance is about the long haul. Yes, there will be set-backs. Muhammad Ali says your success is not measured by how often you get knocked down but by how often you get back up. If you have made a change in the past and have not kept it up, now may be the time to get back up. Getting back up says a lot about the person you are becoming.

START WHERE YOU ARE

Now is the only time that really exists. With the amount of depression and anxiety in the world, it is clear that now is not where we live at all. We are either in the past worrying about things we did wrong or opportunities we missed, or in the future planning, setting goals, and dreaming of *someday*. Someday is today. "As each breath goes out, let it be the end of that moment and the birth of something new," says Buddhist Monk Pema Chödrön. Oh, how I wish it were that easy.

I am a reflective person by nature, so I do a lot of journaling. Reflecting on my old stories and patterns is a way for me to let go. When it comes to the future, that is a different story. I am a planner, so the future is all about checklists and dream circles. Planning is easier when you know where you are going. Where it gets complicated is when I cannot be content in *this* moment. We often look forward to being happy when the boxes are all ticked and the circles are filled. We get stuck in the, "I'll be happy when..." story. Chödrön's book, *Start Where You Are*, challenges that idea. It teaches us how to notice when our mind wanders and to label it "thinking." That's it. We notice. And allow.

Her teaching does not advocate hours of meditative practice. Just simply noticing when we are caught up in *thinking* rather than *being*. This is similar to what I wrote before about being a witness for our thoughts and emotions. The more we can bring our attention to witnessing what is happening in the moment, the easier it is to connect with the present. We can do that by bringing our attention back to our breath—the thing that anchors us in the present. "We cannot breathe in the past or in the future," Chödrön says.

We have a kinship with everything on the planet. When we engage in the practice of noticing and allowing, we can be gentle with ourselves, knowing that we are not alone in our struggle. Western culture is individualistic, so we do not think about interconnectivity very often. Yet, anything you do in your life—how you treat yourself with kindness or harshness, compassion or judgment—will affect how you experience the world. Even greater, it affects the world itself. If you experience feelings or emotions our culture has labeled as negative or bad, breathe them in and connect with them, knowing that somewhere, someone else is experiencing the same thing. Many other people have been where you have been and have experienced the same thing. We have all felt pain. At that moment, if you can connect to others having a similar experience, it can feel much less lonely.

- What if we just listened to what our emotions are trying to tell us?

- What if we were more curious rather than trying to fix and control?

- What is your gut telling you? (We often allow our rational mind to override our gut feelings and intuition.)

Process the feeling instead of passing it on.

Becoming more in tune with our thoughts and emotions—witnessing our self in the present moment—is not a quick solution. It is meant to connect us with ourselves and develop the ability to engage with our lives in a meaningful way. Check back with where you are in the stages of change. There is often resistance to doing something we want to do because it is unfamiliar. Resistance to feeling the thing that is causing you pain is what *actually causes* the pain. It is not necessarily sadness itself, but our resistance to feeling sad. Letting go and opening up can be difficult, so we'll tackle that in an upcoming chapter.

Every moment becomes a memory as soon as we experience it. As soon as we have experienced it, it is gone. Cultivating a daily practice is an opportunity to observe it then hold space for it rather than trying to fix it. Recognizing life experiences—thoughts, emotions, circumstances—as separate from us is the first step in transcending them. We do this by becoming a curious observer in our life. Then, we are free to experience life and thrive regardless of our circumstances.

Who am I when the labels are stripped away?

You are life experiencing itself through you. Witnessing that experience lets life unfold as it will. You witness it outside and inside your sense of self. This is how you thrive. Life is not a problem to be solved. It is not a series of goals you strive towards until you die. Life is passing through you. The real you. The part that is aware of what is happening and allowing yourself to be in the flow. Once we know that all of life passes through us, there are infinite possibilities for what that could be.

REFLECTIVE PRACTICE

Cultivating a WISE Mind

Each one of us has two minds—one is the *rational mind* that focuses on facts and logistics operating from pure reason and the other is the *emotional mind* that reacts to our environment with feelings and sensations in the body. Understanding both our rational and emotional reactions can help us cultivate another way: the wise mind. The wise mind is the ability to balance both the rational and emotional minds and see the world through a new lens entirely.

Begin by simply observing your emotions.

Periodically throughout the day, see if you can recognize what you are feeling and where you are feeling it in your body. For instance, you may feel anxiety in your gut (those butterflies) or through your whole body if it is shaking. You may feel sadness in your throat (being choked up) or as a tightness/heaviness in your chest. Anger can feel explosive, as if it bubbles up from deep down until you "blow your top".

See if you can observe your emotional reactions with curiosity rather than judgment. For example, if someone cuts you off in traffic and road rage explodes from somewhere deep within you, see if you can catch your breath and notice the feeling. How quickly did it happen? Is your heart pounding? Is your body shaking? **Notice.** If you find yourself judging it as an over-reaction, notice that too. Does that critical voice in your head make you feel small? Out of control? Begin simply by observing.

Next is to observe your thoughts.

Sticking with the road rage example, you may notice a string of thoughts that pop in to your head about the experience. When you have a chance to consider the situation more deeply, notice if you have preconceived ideas about different types of drivers. Perhaps you observe thoughts about your own driving. It may be a thought that extends from the experience: "I hate living in the city!" or "Who designed this intersection!?"

Cultivating a wise mind begins by connecting to the emotional mind and the rational mind. You start there. As soon as we are aware of the thoughts and feelings connected to a particular experience, it changes. The wisdom is in connecting these two minds. You can recognize it as the 'aha' insight into the experience you've had. This insight leads to change.

CHAPTER TWO

UNDERSTANDING *Yourself*

How to put down the mask and live authentically

"When we are no longer able to change a situation,
we are challenged to change ourselves."

Viktor Frankl

In my practice as a therapist, I see people struggling and suffering every day. Regardless of the reason for the struggle—death of a loved one, a parent with dementia, loss of a job, a battle with depression or anxiety—people also struggle with how they perceive they are measuring up. When measuring themselves to some invisible standard they or society has set, it is easy to put on a mask to show the world that they are okay. We all seem to be working very hard to convince ourselves and other people that we are. My mask makes me look as if I am coping better than I am, but the mask also makes me feel invisible.

In her book *Broken Open*, Elizabeth Lesser tells the story of 1960's clown-activist Wavy Gravy. His message was that there is no such thing as a bus full of people whose passengers are all thin, healthy, happy, well-dressed and well-liked people belonging to harmonious families who hold jobs that don't bore or aggravate them and who never do anything goofy or mean. Instead, we are all bozos on the bus. Lesser adds to that sentiment by saying we should celebrate that this bus of perfection does not exist. We all struggle from time to time. We all mess up and do not present our best selves. She is encouraging, "If we're all bozos, then for God's sake, we can put down the burden of pretense and get on with being bozos."

This struggle to measure up and fit in is part of the human condition. We all experience it at one time or another. Knowing I am not alone in my suffering or struggle feels hopeful to me. Realizing there is no standard to measure up to is freeing. It frees each of us to honour ourselves, give voice to what we are feeling, and lean a little more deeply into who we are becoming as a result of our life experiences.

THE PLEASURE PARADOX

We have become a society obsessed with perpetual happiness. It has become the benchmark for measuring everything—our mental state, our success, even our world. The World Happiness Report has been ranking 156 countries by their happiness level since 2012. They released their 2016 report on March 2nd and called it World Happiness Day. (Yes, we have a World Happiness Day.) The report believes it reflects a "growing global interest in using happiness and subjective well-being as primary indicators of the quality of human development."

Now, don't get me wrong, *happy* is a great emotion. It is one of my favourites. Labelling it as positive (along with joy and laughter) and others as negative (anger, worry, sadness) is dangerous. It sets us up to want to rid our lives of these "negative" emotions. Then, if we cannot shake them, we label ourselves as deficient in some way.

Our human nature is to feel and process many emotions. We all struggle and feel lost at times. But often, these are the very emotions that lead us to reconsider what is important in our life. A painful event or struggle to make a difficult decision may call us to question. If we find ourselves in this dark night of the soul, that deep internal struggle, it can be an opportunity to deepen our understanding of our self and the world. It may even be the reason you reached for this book. Rather than being a how-to on coping with the chaos of life, I invite you on a journey of self-reflection. It may involve darkness, but the darkness is part of a bigger story.

When we see depression as a negative emotion that interferes with this happiness goal the world has set, our instinct may be to rid ourselves of it rather than lean in and listen to what it has to say. Medication for depression may be part of the healing plan. It was for me when I experienced postpartum depression and could not feel anything. However, when it medicates us into numbness or a blank state of happy, it robs us of the opportunity to dig deeper and question who we are and who we want to become.

Medication was the flashlight that helped me navigate my way out of the darkness leftover from losing two children before having my son. In order to feel love for my new baby, I needed to work my way through the depressive fog. When we measure our lives on our happiness alone, it can feel isolating. If I only evaluated my state of motherhood through the lens of happiness, I would have judged myself to be falling short. I felt joyful for my new baby of course, but I had to make room for the lingering sadness. What I found is that there was space for both.

In terms of the world, what if I live in Denmark (ranked first in the World Happiness Report), should I *always* feel happy? What if I don't? Is there something wrong with me? What if I *do* feel happy, but I live in Burundi (ranked last). Does that mean I'm not empathic to my neighbour's pain? Measuring ourselves and our lives on one emotion may mean judging ourselves harshly when we don't measure up. And, it keeps us focused on our day-to-day feelings rather than on the purpose of our life, which is connected to something bigger than one particular emotion.

Life is complex and sometimes complicated. Grappling with its complexity opens us up to being empathic to others in similar situations or struggles. It is this emotional human connection that leads us to live a meaningful life. Welcoming all feelings and holding space for them in our life unburdens us from chasing happiness day after day. Regardless of the emotion, we can choose to truly appreciate the authenticity of it in the moment and share it with the people closest to us. There is no such thing as an *unmitigated good*. Regardless of what it is we are measuring; there is a point at which it peaks. Then, it declines. *More* is not necessarily *better*.

I believe we know this objectively. Yet, we seem unable to recognize the peak when it comes in our own pursuit of life's pleasures.

The world tells us that the constant pursuit of things (specifically: money, success, power) is not only acceptable, but if we are not hustling every minute of every day to acquire them, we are not doing enough. Slowing down is seen as lazy. If we are not successful in our pursuit, then it is our fault. We must not want it badly enough. This relentless pursuit can become an obsession. We never seem to arrive. We are not satisfied because we do not recognize the sweet spot. We are blindly moving forward so that we do not recognize that happiness isn't waiting on the other side of whatever it is we are chasing. We become frustrated when happiness seems to elude us when we finally arrive.

Have you ever looked at your life and thought: I *should be* happy? Suppose we measure happiness on external acquisitions and status rather than intrinsic feelings of fulfillment and contentment. In that case, we may feel guilty when we are not in a perpetual state of happiness. I am not saying that we should not set goals or pursue things. But, there is no security in a life of constant chasing and striving. In that state, we are like balloons blowing in the wind. We are not anchored to a purpose that is bigger than the pursuit itself. It is void of meaning. What's the point? We often ask the question without really taking the time to consider it. Because we have labelled some pursuits as good and others as bad, we lose sight of the fact that either way, our psyche is affected.

Think about that from the point of view of pursuing things deemed to be bad for us. In any addiction—sex, drugs, food—the rest of our life seems to fall away. We are trapped in the endless pursuit of the next fix. Truth be told: we are a right hot mess constantly chasing the dragon. It is important to step outside the story for a moment to see how hedonistic constantly chasing pleasure really is. Some pleasure in life is good, of course; but, Hedonists believe we should strive for pleasure in an effort to reduce suffering. "Pleasure is good. Pain is bad." Hedonism is the philosophy that focuses on pleasure as the most important pursuit there is for an individual. Whether it is Hedonism (individual pleasure) or Utilitarianism (maximizing pleasure for all people), it leads us to the Pleasure Paradox. That is, when we pursue something, it eludes us. We cannot acquire it directly.

Happiness and pleasure are the reason we strive for anything, when you think about it. Money, success, power are the things we believe will make us happy. We set our sights on a big house, fancy vacations, and fast cars but are not satisfied when we get them. Iris Mauss is an assistant professor in psychology at the University of Denver whose research focuses on happiness, stress, and mental health. She says, "If you explicitly and purposely focus on happiness, that appears to have a self-defeating quality." She concluded that women focused on happiness may set higher standards and judge themselves harshly when they fall short. She also found that focusing on individual happiness led to a breakdown in personal relationships, resulting in feeling unhappy.

The Death of Ivan Ilyich was a short novel written by Leo Tolstoy in the 1870s when he was grappling with questions of morality, mortality, and meaning in his own life. At just 45 years old, the protagonist Ivan knew he was going to die. As we are compelled to do when faced with death, Ilyich reviewed his life. By all accounts, he had done well. Professionally, he studied law and became a judge. He had achieved high social standing and wealth, mostly because he was obsessed with it—always in pursuit, constantly climbing upward. Before he dies, he reflects on his life and realizes, too late, that his life was not one of pleasure or happiness at all. Rather, he had spent most of his adult life unconsciously pursuing the things society deemed important. On his deathbed, he is confronted with the ultimate question about life: Was it meaningful?

Living a meaningful life is about connecting to something bigger than the constant pursuit of pleasure and happiness. Happiness is an emotion. It is fleeting. Joy, contentment, peace and purpose, however, are more tangible. Rather than an emotion, they are states of being. The vehicle you travel in rather than the destination.

- What brings you joy (contentment, peace, purpose)?

- When do you feel the most content? (Contentment usually comes as a result of feeling connected to something bigger than yourself.)

- What are your talents, and how do you share them with the world?

- How do you serve the people around you? (There is nothing more fulfilling than being of service.)

ADDICTED TO BUSY

Busy has become a socially acceptable addiction. Our world moves so fast, and our success is measured on our productivity within it. How often do you answer "busy" to the question, "How are you?" The asker then nods and moves on. There's an understanding. We're all so busy all the time. When we answer busy, what we're really trying to say is that we are successful. If we are busy, we must be doing something meaningful to contribute to the world. The problem is that busy can be a way of distracting us from the things that are deep and meaningful. Disconnection and addiction often travel together, according to Gabor Maté, an MD on the West Coast of Canada who specializes in addiction as a response to trauma.

When we go a mile-a-minute, we don't have time to slow down and look in the mirror. "Is this the life I imagined?", "Is my relationship healthy?", "Am I living a purpose-filled life?" As long as we keep moving, we do not have to interact with these questions. We live behind a mask because looking too deeply into our lives may scare us. Asking life's big question and taking time to be reflective may feel unsettling. So, we dodge these existential questions by keeping busy. Thinking about anything other than the task in front of us may mean we have to do something different. For example, slowing down may lead to the realization that we need a shift in perspective or to challenge society's stranglehold on our life. It can be painful to see how far from our values we are living.

Mindfulness is a practice of being in the present moment—being fully present to what you are doing rather than what you are thinking. We move so fast, running to keep up and judging ourselves along the way for not doing enough, not doing things perfectly, not achieving as much as our peers or measuring up to societal standards. Rather than doing a hundred things where we give a fraction of our self, why not pick a few meaningful things and go deep? Parents of young children may get caught up in the busyness of the day-to-day—just getting them clothed, fed, and put to bed can leave even the most energetic parent feeling exhausted.

Slowing down and really considering the world we are creating for future generations may scare the bejesus out of us. Have you ever con-templated this as you've watched your sleeping child? Yes, it's scary. But asking the question can help us make space for those things that will have a critical impact long-term. It opens us up to living today in a way that creates the tomorrow we envision. Being busy keeps us spinning our wheels, always in such a rush to get things done. That said, have you ever noticed that time speeds up the faster you move? Will I get all the activities and responsibilities managed before the end of the week, the end of the month? Will I beat-the-clock?

In the quiet moments, when I am fully immersed in one thing, time seems to follow my lead. It slows down to meet me where I am. If you were to look at your whole life in an hourglass, how would you feel seeing the sands of time moving as fast as you move? I think I would do whatever it takes to slow them down. Otherwise, my life would feel as if it were slipping away from me.

Moving so fast, being so busy, I cannot appreciate it fully. On our deathbed, we all want more time to do the things that we consider meaningful. In the end, we may look back to see we did not take the time to do these things. Doing more of the things we love and being fully present in the moment would have brought more feelings of fulfillment. A life lived intentionally, time spent on the things that mattered most. Typically, those are not the things we are doing when we say *busy*.

Of course, we all have responsibilities—jobs, businesses, children, parents and staff—depending upon us. Finding the time to slow down means making difficult decisions. It means prioritizing and setting things down that are unimportant in the long run. Pacing ourselves is a practice that we engage in every day, with every commitment and activity. Bringing in a practice of mindfulness can be the first step in slowing down. Rather than scheduling time in our day to practice mindfulness, we can bring mindfulness into each task. For example, bring mindfulness to a mundane task like washing dishes by noticing the warmth of the water, the smell of the bubbles, the trees outside the window (if you have a window).

Bring your five senses into each experience—what do you see, hear, feel, smell, taste? Not every experience will have every element, but focus on what is happening at that precise moment in time. Bring your mind back to the moment whenever you notice it wandering back to ruminate on something that's happened or when it's jumping ahead to all the "what if" worries in the future.

When we are living from this wise mind, it is easier to decide which things to put down and which things to devote our time to doing. As you cultivate your wise mind, be aware of the distractions that steal large chunks of time but contribute nothing of significance to your well-being. Of course, not everything you do needs to make your heart sing, but you should be able to hear a mild hum. The hum is hope. It's what keeps you connected to your life's purpose so that you do not run out of time before it is fulfilled.

MAKING SPACE

When the Netflix series *Tidying Up* with Marie Kondo was released in 2019, it seemed everyone I knew was in the midst of purging their homes with the KonMari method for organizing. For many people, tidying up not only means taking the time to unload the old junk from the basement. It can also mean considering your life from a different perspective, reconsidering that old bias you inherited, making space for new ideas. The KonMari method is quite prescribed and has you going through things by category rather than room-by-room. The biggest difference: you do not simply consider the usefulness of an object (rational mind); you also consider keeping only the things that spark joy in your life (emotional mind).

Charlie's Story

"How do I know what sparks joy in my stuff when I have no idea what sparks joy in me?" Charlie's adult children had been dropping hints about cleaning up his house since his wife Ellie died last year. The *Tidying Up* movement had taken the suggestions to a new level. The kids were not wrong, Charlie's house had become a bit unmanageable since Ellie had taken care of much of the housework throughout their 43 years together. Charlie sought my help with finding a routine and strategies that would help him organize. He told me he felt fairly certain that he had handled the emotional stuff quite well, "all things considered". Certainly, I could help him craft a plan to clean, but I wondered why he called a grief therapist for support and not a home organizer.

In addition to the logistics of cleaning and organizing, Charlie needed support working through the memories. In order to consider the things that would bring him joy, he needed to make space for the joy. When he came to see me, he wondered if he'd ever feel joy again. What he knew for certain was that the joy was not going to come from holding his vacuum cleaner. Making space in our physical surroundings—home or office—can feel great. Life is easier when we know where stuff is, or "where it lives", as my sister would say. Being able to navigate easily in our physical space can help us feel more in control of our life.

Most cleaning is about physical stuff rather than an emotional tidying up, however. Finding space in your heart requires different work. Does your heart feel cluttered? It's not as easy to determine as looking at the space in our homes. When our hearts are full of old grudges, past hurts, painful memories, those things will never spark a joyful life. Worse, they can make it difficult for joyful experiences to come in. There is no space. Emotional tidying up includes things like working through an exercise in forgiveness—letting go of the things in your life that no longer serve you and reframing your memories so that you focus on what you learned rather than what happened. Like the heart, it is not always easy to recognize when your soul needs attention. It's like that junk drawer we all have; soul work is often the last thing we consider. If you never open it, the prospect of cleaning it up can be very scary. You may have no idea what you will find.

I believe our soul contains the essence of who we are. It is the foundation of how we live our lives. Our soul gives us that gut-level feeling when we are making decisions about our life. Have you ever experienced a feeling of uneasiness for seemingly no good reason? That's your soul talking—your intuition. Our souls require that we pay attention to the things that make us who we are: our values, beliefs, and principles.

- What is my purpose?

- Who am I?

- Who am I here for?

These are soul questions.

Talking about his approach to cleaning the house made jumping into grief work a sensible extension for Charlie. It was more than just space in the house he needed to focus on. It was also space in his heart so he could feel love, and space in his soul so he could experience grace. The first step was to find some reinforcements to help. His daughters were delighted to help with the house. For his emotional work, he committed to therapy and to joining a support group for grievers. Together, we focused on working through things that felt unfinished with his wife. As we talked about his relationship, it was easy for Charlie to find places where he felt he made a mess of things. He needed someone to hear his apology for the times he felt he let Ellie down. Identifying places where he needed to forgive her shortcomings was more difficult.

Charlie had been brought up with the adage of not speaking ill of the dead. If he were honest, there were some places in their relationship where Ellie may have sought his forgiveness for mistakes she had made. Looking at it that way, he imagined her asking for forgiveness and was much more able to extend it. Forgiveness does not mean the other person is off the hook for bad behaviour. It is simply a decision that you will let go of the hold it has in your relationship, or in Charlie's case, his heart and his memories. When it comes to forgiveness issues, we need to be aware of the residue it can leave—shame and guilt. Brené Brown is a leading researcher in the area of shame. Our resistance to feeling shame can hold us hostage. It is uncomfortable. If we are going to be vulnerable with one another, however, we have to take risks. Risks mean messing up.

In her book, *Daring Greatly*, Brown says the way to connect is learning to be vulnerable and risking shame. "Vulnerability is the core of all emotions and feelings. To feel is to be vulnerable...Vulnerability is the birthplace of love, belonging, joy, courage, empathy, accountability, and authenticity. If we want greater clarity in our purpose or deeper and or meaningful spiritual lives, vulnerability is the path." We are social creatures, experiencing life in relation—to the world, to one another, and to our self. Honouring our own growth, even the messy bits, opens us up to being more vulnerable with others. Learning to witness our own pain and suffering means we can witness it in other people as well. There is something powerful in having our pain witnessed and our voice heard. It is the key to healing our hearts.

BREAKING THE PATTERNS

The emotional work can be difficult and long, which is why we may put it off. We tend to think that we procrastinate simply because we do not want to tackle the task at hand, but that is not always the case. Avoiding a task is a way to put things off because we fear failure or success. Perhaps we are decisional procrastinators—deciding not to decide, to stay in our comfort zone where it is nice and safe.

Wanting to do things perfectly can be an excuse to stay stuck. Perfection cannot complete a task unless certain of success, so it befriends Procrastination. When you think about it, these two are made for each other. Procrastination does not have to act if Perfection keeps jumping in with all the "what if's" and "OMG's." When Procrastination begins to think about getting up and doing something, Perfection says wait. If we think about Procrastination and Perfection as best friends, there is a technique we can apply for success. The first step is awareness, you cannot fix a problem if you do not recognize it. Look for patterns in your life that are holding you back from the results you want. My desire for a healthy body and my passion for crunchy, salty things are often in competition. If I look closely, it is often my desire to be perfect in my eating patterns that will call on Procrastination. As long as I put off healthy eating by eating chips every night, there is the possibility of eating perfectly, eventually.

Perfection is a state of flawlessness or supreme excellence. Perfection is static; life is not. Life moves from one experience to another, fluidly. Procrastination is usually associated with fear of failure. If the destination is not clear or seems unattainable, procrastinating is an action word. "Do something else", Procrastination whispers to us. Whether you think you'll fail or you feel undeserving of success, Procrastination keeps us right where we are. Pushing through it starts with becoming familiar with your personal brand of procrastination. Our rational mind knows what we need to do. Our emotional mind keeps us from doing it. The wise mind says—make a list, recognize the patterns, set a small and measurable goal to move you from here to there.

Where are your struggles? What are the underlying emotions that go with the struggles? Our natural tendency is towards entropy. In physics, it is the flow of energy that increases over time. The universe tends to move towards a state of disorder. It takes a lot of energy to pull things back from a state of chaos. Think about that in the context of housework. We need to work on things constantly to keep them in a state of order. That means, if you want to break the patterns of procrastination and perfection, you need to establish new patterns of interacting.

Overcoming procrastination begins with awareness. In the stages of change it looks like going from pre-contemplation, where you are not serious about changing or even admitting there is a problem, to contemplation. You may see yourself moving from defending your patterns to seeing them as a problem, or at the very least, considering changing behaviour or breaking patterns. You still don't know what to do, but you decide you want to change at this stage.

Stage two is about restructuring and preparing for change. It is really easy to get stuck here. Especially if we are battling perfectionism or self-doubt. You may know what you need to do to change but are afraid. Staying stuck in your old patterns may be uncomfortable, but at least it is familiar and safe. Jumping straight from contemplation to action is dangerous too. It could lead to failure and push you straight back to the beginning. I heard it said recently that perfection is uncertainty with lipstick. Is it really fear? Fear is often the thing leading us away from our best-laid plans for reflection and growth. Take time here to examine what could happen if you try and fail. What might be the emotions that come from that? How will you handle setbacks and all-or-nothing thinking? How are you going to measure your success?

Now you have a plan that can move you towards action. We know you cannot depend on willpower to move you forward. One of the biggest challenges with action is that we think about stopping something rather than replacing it with something else. For example, Procrastination may be convincing me I can go to the gym later or give up chips next week. It is harder when I have an appointment with a personal trainer and have to share my food journal. Putting the plan in action and getting traction is where a new storyline begins to take shape, and we become resilient in the face of adversity and challenge.

BECOMING RESILIENT

Life can be challenging. Struggle does not depend on whether or not you are a good person. You can do the right things and keep a positive attitude, but that does not mean that life will never knock you on your ass. Believing that life will be fair because you are a good person is like believing the bull won't charge at you because you are a vegetarian. Resilience is about learning to navigate difficult life circumstances by understanding where your strength lies.

There has been a lot written in recent years about resilience in the face of life's challenges. Institutes have been set up, and studies have been conducted, but what is resilience, really? The dictionary defines resilience as the ability to spring back into shape. From a human perspective, it is our capacity to recover quickly from life's challenges and difficulties. Managing our way through difficult situations and stressors can lead to new knowledge about situations and strengthen our confidence in our ability to overcome obstacles. In fact, continuing to overcome life's challenges can lead to trusting ourselves as we realize that we can overcome, endure, and maybe even become stronger because of the adversity we have faced.

Of course, you will never know if you are a resilient person unless you have gone through at least one difficult situation. Becoming a resilient person means challenging how we interpret the events that happen in our life. Do we label them as traumatic, or do we see them as an opportunity to learn and grow? Events are not traumatic in and of themselves. Rather, it is our reaction to an event that determines whether or not it is traumatic and what wounds it leaves. This is why children growing up in the same set of circumstances may have very different reactions. It is the interpretation of the event(s) that dictate how the individual will move through any given situation. Reactions to events can be internal or external depending on how we see the situation and how we feel about our self. For example, some people will think: "This situation is happening to me because I am not a good person". Others will think: "This situation is the result of something happening in my environment; how will I overcome it?"

The time to strengthen our resilience is during calm times in our life. We do this by talking about how we *feel*, not just what we think. That includes the messy stuff we no longer label as negative: grief, anger, loneliness. It means taking more responsibility for ourselves and our lives by reflecting on challenges as they come up and adapting quickly. It means attending to significant relationships in our lives by sharing love, being kind, being present and empathetic. Our best hope for resilience is to be strengthening our support systems all the time. One way to build resilience is to remember the times in your life when you have overcome adversity and became stronger after the experience. Each time life throws a curveball, we have the opportunity to challenge our assumptions. The strength of the human spirit comes from tackling those assumptions and moving through them by creating a path you would never have had the opportunity to travel otherwise.

FINDING OUR AUTHENTIC SELF

The more we understand our selves and our patterns, the easier it is to build resilience. In any given situation, we may hear a multitude of voices in our heads, all speaking at the same time. I have always wondered: "Which voice is the real me? Am I the one talking or the one listening? Am I the one judging or the one feeling judged?" Taking that line of questioning a little further, I wonder: "Is it possible that I am both the person listening *and* the one talking? Is it possible that I am neither?"

Who we are goes beyond what is happening in our mind, it goes deeper than the voices in our head, and it also goes beyond how we feel. For example, I can be happy, and I can be sad; neither says anything about who I am. It is simply how I am feeling (internal) in any given situation (external). I am more than just my feelings, just as I am more than my thoughts or physical body.

There are three interdependent realms necessary for helping us discover and connect to our authentic self: the physical (body), intellectual (mind) and spiritual (soul). The *real me* exists somewhere in the middle, like a Venn diagram of sorts. I exist at the point where all three intersect. Looking inward to connect with our authentic self includes connecting to the world through all three realms. If we can appreciate ourselves from all three perspectives—mind, body, spirit—it may help quiet the thoughts and feelings that fight for our attention and leave us feeling utterly confused about how to move forward.

Our authentic self does not identify with only one thought or feeling in particular. It goes beyond the thoughts in our head or what we are feeling at any particular moment. It is deeper than our day-to-day experiences. The underlying theory in narrative therapy, and telling our story, is that we are experts in our own lives. We speak our lives into existence (what you think, you are). Our lives are our stories.

The idea of accepting ourselves when our circumstances are not exactly how we would like them may seem ludicrous. Yet, self-acceptance is exactly what each of us needs to move towards self-love. Thinking we are incomplete or less than leads to feelings of pain and holds you back from loving yourself through the difficult parts of life's journey.

In her book, *I Know I'm In There Somewhere*, Helene Brenner describes it as "something you experience when you discover that you can pay attention to your innermost feelings and desire with care and compassion." Brenner begins by uncovering what our inner voice is and how to distinguish it from outside voices. The inner voice (or self) is not just what you consciously experience. It is also what you feel, sense, and want from life. Think: passion and purpose. The challenge is in aligning your inner and outer self—what we may think about as the soul and the ego—so that you experience a state of harmony.

We often learn to align ourselves with culture, friends and family to create this harmony because we want to fit in and belong. But think about how society raises women—be polite, friendly, and attuned to the needs of others, often sacrificing personal needs and desires. Girls are punished for being smart or outspoken, which can lead to losing our connection to our inner voice. Connecting to our inner voice, our authentic self, is what you may think of as an *aha!* moment. You may not even be able to explain it, yet you know it is true for you. It feels really good to be in alignment with yourself in that way. There may even be a feeling of knowing what to do next or a feeling that you have remembered something.

Understanding your authentic self is what begins to emerge as you spend more time experiencing your life from a wise mind. Staying in the present moment by being aware of your thoughts and emotions helps to uncover patterns in the story you may feel do not fit authentically into who you are becoming. Understanding all the parts of our self is helpful. Have you ever been invited to an event only to find that one part of you wants to go and another part wants to stay home? We have lots of parts—the young, free-spirited part of me may be the part who wants to go have fun. The self-conscious part, that often emerges in our teen years, may be the part who wants to avoid awkward conversations and embarrassing situations.

Humans are complex, multi-dimensional beings. There are times in our lives we feel strong and capable and other times we feel completely unprepared. We have been loved and hurt. Every event in our lives, accompanied by our thoughts and feelings about that event, stands as a snap-shot in time. The person we were at the time of the event is not the person we are today. Memorable events create a strong sense of self in that moment and that self can live on in our minds, almost like characters in a story. Each of these moments are part of who we are, parts that make up our sense of self. Getting to know these parts, finding compassion for what that part went through, and healing old wounds are all necessary for healing and a feeling of wholeness.

While Sigmund Freud may have identified our parts as id, ego, and superego, Richard Schwartz sees it as more complex than that. As a family therapist, Schwartz saw the family as a system and worked with the individuals within that system. The way we understand ourselves from the time we are born is in relation to another. As infants, we understand ourselves and the world in relation to our primary caregivers. As children, it is the family. Teens extend to peers; young adults to their partners or colleagues, and so on. How we understand our self is similar. Externally it can be in relation to the roles we play and the people around us. Internally it is in relation to the parts of us we may still be able to recognize—parts that were hurt, parts that feel uncertain, parts that had success. Our authentic self is like the family system for all these individual parts. Harmony within the self (or the system) is achieved by getting all the parts moving together towards a specific goal. I think of it like a flock of birds or a school of fish—many individual parts all moving harmoniously as one.

This can be difficult with parts of our self that have been injured and may be unwilling or unable to integrate. We will explore that more in the upcoming chapter on healing trauma. For now, the key in understanding our self is knowing we are made up of different parts, all connected to various times and stories in our lives and that it is possible to experience peace and calm within the system.

REFLECTIVE ACTIVITY

Sketching the Story of your Life

Understanding your self comes from considering who you are from many perspectives. As a visual person, you may want to sketch or use colour as you consider the following questions. If you journal, you can use that. This type of creative exercise taps into a part of the brain we want to activate and cultivate.

Roots: these are your values. When life is stormy, what keeps you anchored? Is it particular people? A sense of security? Your faith? An independent, resilient spirit? The roots may not be completely formed. Some roots may be bigger than others. Ask yourself: "What are the things that ground me?"

Trunk: these are your skills. They are the characteristics that define you, not just a list on your resume of things you can do. Are you an active listener? A trusted confidante? Do you have a strong work ethic? Are you organized, or can you pull things together in a crisis? Your values are more about who you are, your character. Your skills are the characteristics that bring your character to life through your daily interactions and activities.

Branches: these are your hopes and desires. Branches are ways in which you stretch yourself. Branches are about becoming. Manifestations of your values. They will often grow in particular directions if provided with structure and pruning. Branches contain dreams for your family, your health and your career. How much time and energy do you want to devote to each?

Blossoms/Fruit: these are the successes in your life. What would your hopes and dreams look like if they were to bloom fully? Often, we forget to enjoy the fruits of our labour. We can get so caught up in the maintenance of the tree (or our life) that we miss the harvest—the blessings.

Seeds: these are the things you want to leave behind. Your legacy. Your epilogue. Seeds are the basis for other trees, coming generations. What are the values you want to pass on? Are you making an impact in the areas of life that are meaningful to you? Seeds are the things you plant in the world.

CHAPTER THREE

HOLDING *Space*

How to slow down and trust the process

"A healer does not heal you. A healer is someone who holds space for you while you awaken your inner healer, so that you may heal yourself."

Maryam Hasnaa

People need to feel loved and accepted where they are now. Sometimes the present feels uncomfortable, which is often what brings people into therapy. It may not be one particular issue that has brought a person to this particular juncture in life. Rather, it may be a culmination of events that leaves a person feeling frustrated, confused, or just plain stuck. As a therapist, I see my role as being with people where they are at that moment in time—without judgment, without pretext, and without trying to fix the situation. However, we are a culture that deeply desires to fix or improve. We give advice and offer support to help a person change either the situation or the self. There seems to be little room for just being who or where we are.

Just being in the moment, with whatever emotion or thought that has come up, is what it means to hold space. Rather than judging, or problem-solving, or hurrying to the next thing we think we ought to be doing, we simply stay in the moment and experience everything that is happening in that space. We can hold space for ourselves and for others. The key is being in the space together—observing, witnessing what is happening. The thing I like about holding space is learning to trust our wisdom—that we will know what to do when the time comes. We can also learn to love our self and others in any given situation, with relationships transcending the circumstances.

It is helpful to be quiet, listen, and notice what is happening during these moments. That may feel uncomfortable or unnatural if we do not have a lot of experience being still in this way. We tend to want to control our emotions and manage our behaviour. And, while that may be part of the process eventually, it is not always helpful when you're getting started. Wanting to move out of the space you are in reinforces the idea that where we are at this point in time is wrong. If it is wrong, we will desperately want to get away and move forward. Learning to sit with that discomfort builds resilience and helps you find clarity in the present.

CONNECTING WITH EMOTIONS

Imagine you feel angry and you no longer want to feel that way so often. You set a goal to stop being angry. Then, inevitably, something happens and you feel angry again. In addition to feeling angry about the situation, you then feel angry at yourself for *being* angry.

Next, imagine that instead of trying to control the angry feeling, you just quietly observed it instead. With *curiosity*. Without judgment, pretext, control, or trying to fix the situation or your reaction to it. Just observing the feeling and allowing it to run its course can move us away from judging the feeling (or ourselves for having it), as we have talked about in the previous chapters.

Now, you are holding space.

Holding space for yourself means learning to love yourself right where you are in *this moment*, regardless of circumstance. It is believing you are deserving of love, empathy, and acceptance. Holding space moves us from our heads (problem-solving) to our hearts (unconditional love). This is contrary to our self-improvement culture of the past fifty years. Just for a moment, imagine a world where each day, regardless of our own personal circumstances, we all showed up, just as we are, and simply loved one another. It would change the whole world.

Holding Space for Anger

Introducing the idea of holding space for ourselves and others sounds like a simple thing to do. It is part of a mindfulness practice which we are constantly being encouraged to adopt. It may be easier to hold space for situations that involve celebration, but what about emotions and situations we have been taught are negative. Anger is one of those emotions for women. As far back as I can remember, there was an unspoken rule that *nice girls don't get angry.* Imagine my surprise when anger showed up in my dream one night and told me her name was Margaret. She was tall and fat and very angry. In the dream, I was taking her to therapy. When I woke up, I realized Angry Fat Girl was a part of me. I had gained weight being pregnant for nearly three years trying to have my son. Although I knew I needed to lose weight, I had no energy for it. Even when I did try, I didn't seem to get any results and I felt stuck.

Angry Fat Girl, which I call her affectionately, surprised me. Not the fat part—that was obvious—but the anger. Growing up in a traditional Christian faith, being a nice girl came with lots of underlying and overt messages about how I was supposed to think and behave. When I came face to face with the fact that my excess weight was related to anger, I was shocked. I didn't *feel* angry.

A few months after my dream, I had the opportunity to try hypnotherapy to see if I could jump-start my weight loss. As the doctor visually guided me down the stairs into a boardroom, he said everyone sitting around the table was there to sign a contract that would support my weight loss efforts. Out of the corner of my eye, I could see Angry Fat

Girl. Her face said it all, "Whatever. I'll sign it, but I ain't doing it!" After my session, I gained another seven pounds.

In the second hypnotherapy session, the doctor guided me down into a large room where there was a party. There was a smaller room off to the side that held the resistance to my weight loss efforts. I knew when I unlocked the door I'd find Angry Fat Girl. What I did not anticipate was that she would be huddled in the corner crying. Immediately, I went over to hug her and told her I'd help her. Right then it hit me. In my selfish desire to lose weight, I had forgotten her. I had forgotten the part of the dream where I was taking her to therapy.

A few months later, I had the opportunity to attend a therapeutic counselling workshop teaching a technique called Empty Chair. It requires you to put two chairs facing one another. You take turns occupying both chairs and speaking for yourself and the other person, or the part of yourself that is keeping you stuck. It is a helpful exercise when you feel as if you cannot speak to someone directly. This technique is especially helpful in both grief and trauma healing work. In my case, I worked with the part of me that was not moving towards a common goal and was becoming a barrier in my life. It was not the weight but the emotions under it that I needed to heal.

I let Angry Fat Girl speak first. "What am I supposed to do with my anger if I can't eat?" she barked. It was a fair question. Earlier I mentioned that I did not feel angry. By that I mean I did not feel it in my body—no obvious tension, tightness, or shaky feeling that is a clue anger is taking up space. There were no obvious thoughts or feelings of being angry like raging and complaining, except when I focused on my weight. Angry Fat Girl was a part of me that had been born to take on that burden. Eating was a way to numb the thoughts and feelings and keep them from seeping in to my conscious mind where I'd have to deal with them. Numbing is a way of keeping all that deep down, under the surface.

It was in that Empty Chair session where Angry Fat Girl and the part of me that was witnessing her agreed to work together. She told me that the weight she was carrying was to let the world know I was not okay. Angry Fat Girl had been the voice for a slew of emotions I needed to work through. I was carrying grief, frustration, and loneliness from the stillborn children I had carried and given birth to. Unconsciously I thought, "What would people think if I was thin and healthy and seemed to have my life together?" Those unconscious thoughts and emotions I could not feel became a burden she carried as an extra fifty pounds on my body. A silent voice screaming to the world, "I am not OK." Her voice was angry that other people abandoned me in those painful moments.

The weight came off once I came to terms with those thoughts and feelings and did some grief work around my losses. That involved talking to other people about my experience and asking them to be there with me as I cried or yelled about how unfair it all seemed to be. I've come to have such love and compassion for the part of me that manifested as Angry Fat Girl. She helped me notice my emotions and how to give them a voice by asking her, "Why are you here? Is there anything I can do to help?" Most times, when we ask a part of our self this question, the answer is simply to be present and hold space for that part, even if it feels uncomfortable.

Have you experienced *nice girls don't get angry* in your life? For boys and young men, it may have been that anger was the only emotion you felt permitted to show. Perhaps there are other messages that came directly or indirectly from the church, school, parents, or society. There are many subconscious messages that are the undertone growing up. Because I did not feel or express anger in a healthy way, a part of me took on my burden. She was my protector—plowing through bag after bag of crunchy, salty, aggression food that kept me numb. She was not very cooperative when I asked her to help me lose weight. She did not know how I would cope without overeating as a way of pushing down painful emotions.

Harriet Lerner writes about this in her book *The Dance of Anger*. She says the challenge is that anger appears as a signal you need to listen to. "Our anger may tell us that we are not addressing an important emotional issue in our lives, or that too much of our self—our beliefs, values, desires, or ambitions—is being compromised in a relationship." Of course, I thought anger would look like anger if I ever experienced it. It didn't. For me, Angry Fat Girl was simply the voice for other emotions that left me feeling vulnerable. She was the protector of grief, loneliness, abandonment.

CULTIVATING SPACE FOR CARING

As the firstborn in a family of four kids, I took on the role of little mother very early. In fact, I would say I was my youngest brother's primary emotional caregiver for most of his young life. If there was conflict or discomfort in our family, I wanted to rescue everyone. I did not like conflict, so I kept the peace by taking care of everyone's needs. Watching someone struggle made me feel so insecure that I went about trying to fix everything and making everyone happy. Harmony felt like safety. That role then extended to my life beyond my family where I was caretaker to all my friends.

At work, I wanted to please my superiors, usually in an effort to feel secure in my job. Of course, the social justice side of me was also very strong. I like things to be fair. Fair meant everyone was happy so there was less conflict. I often found myself in a battle when these two things did not align. Halfway through her book on anger, Lerner states, "When we do not put our primary emotional energy into solving our own problems, we take on other people's problems as our own." If I were honest with myself, I grew up trying to solve everyone else's problems to keep the peace. People came to me and I would spring to action. It never occurred to me that I could simply make space for the other person's struggle without doing anything beyond listening and caring.

It was often difficult for me, especially in my childhood, to see where I stopped and the people around me began. My emotions seemed to depend on how the other person felt. If someone was struggling, I felt uncomfortable. Getting clear on what was mine and what was another person's took expanding the space so there was room for both. Making space and identifying these patterns in relationships helps us understand the steps in the dance. The steps of this dance are familiar—you move this way, I move that way. The steps are our habits, and inevitably, we will fall back into old patterns from time to time even when we try to switch things up.

Making space for a new dance means we can move more freely. You can have your issues and emotions and I can have mine. We can talk together. Cry together. Heal together. We are not so close that I get overwhelmed by your stuff or you get overwhelmed by mine. There is space. We are in there together. The dance is an analogy for movement and patterns. The more space we have, the easier it is to move. Old patterns limit how we do that so it is important to always be exploring how they may halt movement towards healing.

Holding Space for Loneliness

Who are your people? The ones you go to when you need support or feel alone, who lift you up when you are down, who hold you together when you feel broken? We ALL need people. We understand ourselves and our world in relation. We witness for one another, process emotions together and problem-solve so we can live more in our wise mind. Our world, especially in the West, has become fragmented. A great deal of emphasis is put on individual achievement. We claim our success as ours alone. Likewise, our schools and businesses are more competitive than collaborative. Yet, we have survived as a species because we have worked together. We cannot continue to be pulled apart in competition.

We all have basic needs for survival and growth. Abraham Maslow postulated that our survival and safety needs are basic needs for humanity. Without these, we cannot reach higher levels of growth. Belonging sits in the middle of this hierarchy. These are our psychological needs—love, intimacy, relationship. The idea is that community and supporting one another is necessary for us to move beyond. Our growth needs are at the top of the pyramid and include achievement or accomplishment in life. Maslow says our growth needs are less about the self. We typically think of self-esteem as our own positive regard for our self; however, it is actually more about dignity, mastery, and respect for others.

Everything up to the point of our growth needs is referred to as a deficiency need. If we do not have the basics, including love and mastery of self, we cannot move to the highest level, which is self-actualization. This is our desire "to become everything one is capable of becoming," according to Maslow. Of course, more levels and layers have been added to this theory over the years—cognitive, aesthetic, spiritual—but the basic premise is that we cannot move to higher levels until we meet the needs that precede it.

With all due respect to Maslow, I believe our need for love and belonging to be a biological or physiological need rather than a psychological one. It is the underpinning of humanity. It is the reason we stretch ourselves to higher levels. To be of service to others and to make the world a better place is our legacy. It is more foundational than it appears in the hierarchy of needs. In the early 20th century, stories about death rates amongst children in orphanages showed that in most cases their deaths were not due to a lack of basic needs. The children were fed, medicated, and safe but they lacked love. These stories showed that the children needed touch and physical affection to live. If they did happen to live with a lack of physical touch, those who survived were severely limited in cognitive and psychological function. *Failure to thrive* is still a term used for babies lacking emotional stimulation. These kids just stop growing and progressing. The Surgeon General says the same is true for adults. He considers isolation the most common disease in western societies.

According to Gabor Maté, the state of addiction today is also connected to a lack of love and connection. He says, "Only in the presence of compassion will people see the truth." Our world is always going to be filled with difficulties. Relationships are complicated; humans are flawed and our systems are imperfect. We struggle and fail and fall. Our bodies break down. We have our own internal demons to quiet, especially when childhoods have been less than perfect, which is all of us. Healing comes from knowing you are not alone, that other people are going through the same struggle. I love how Pema Chödrön puts it, "Compassion becomes real when we recognize our shared humanity." Knowing we are not alone in our struggle makes it easier somehow. Like our values, our relationships with our fellow humans are roots that ground us.

When my client's mom died recently, she asked her friends to sit right up front. As close to the family section as possible so that when she was the most vulnerable, she could look to them for support. She could turn her head and know she was not alone. She belonged to a community of women who loved her through her pain. Who are the people you rely on for that sense of love and belonging? If you cannot identify them right away, you may need to find them. With new communities focused on belonging and sharing popping up all over, they are out there. We cannot survive alone, which is why I see this need as fundamental to our survival.

Love and belonging are what move us towards spiritual growth. We hold one another up and witness for each other as we learn to witness for ourselves. Love is an extension of our self. M. Scott Peck says that, "Among humanity, love is the miraculous force that defies the natural law of entropy." It is how we work together collectively to bring order to the universe. It is how we evolve towards higher states of consciousness.

Melina's Story

Melina described herself as a loner. Her dad left when she was a small child and she never really saw him again. As her mother tried to pull her life together, Melina and her brother were often left in the care of their grandmother. Once, when left with her grandmother for an entire year, the resentment of having to step back into a primary caregiver role caused her grandmother to take her feelings out on Melina. She expected, as the older female child, that Melina would take on a lot of the responsibility, despite her young age. Melina worked hard to try and please her grandmother, who berated her and called her names—fat, lazy, stupid. We all have voices in our head, internal dialogue and for Melina, it was her grandmother's voice continuously telling her she was unworthy. It is no wonder Melina saw being unlovable as her character flaw. She saw loneliness as her fault—she was alone because she was difficult to love.

Melina entered therapy because she was struggling with anxiety and neglecting herself and it was showing up in her work life. She also wanted a relationship, but the idea seemed far beyond her reach. So many years of loneliness had made the idea of love and belonging something she could not imagine. "Who could love someone like her?" Studies show evidence that heart disease and premature death are two times higher in female patients who report feeling lonely. It is even higher for men. Men who reported feeling lonely were three times more likely to be experiencing anxiety and depression. Like Melina, people who feel anxious or depressed may not feel capable of being around other people. Yet, as social beings, being alone is a high risk. Because our natural tendency is to love people in the language that makes us feel loved, it may make us feel disconnected in our relationships if we are not loved in the way we can feel it.

Melina had no idea how to feel loved when we met. Finding a community was a goal she had set but it was way outside her comfort zone. In the spirit of growth and healing, however, Melinda joined a small choir. She liked the idea of blending in by focusing on her part—her voice blending with other voices and creating something harmonious. After a few practices, the idea of not going and spending time with *her people* was not an option. It turns out, spending quality time with people who loved what she loved was exactly what she needed. She loved the experience and the people she met. It took a little longer for her to believe that these new people could really love her. The more time she spent with them, the less alone and anxious she felt. That opened her up to being able to receive love. It also challenged her beliefs. If these people could love her, she must be lovable. Although it felt a little weird at first, it became more comfortable with practice (and commitment).

If you identify with Melina, start small. Work with someone to find the strength you need to reach out and find your people. If you know someone who is isolated, reach out to them. We are human, and human emotions can be complex. We all feel awkward at times. It helps to remember we are all on this crazy journey of life together.

ANXIETY & DEPRESSION: TWO SIDES OF THE SAME COIN

Holding Space for Anxiety

"Can you make it go away?" my client asked me. She was talking about her anxiety which seemed to be getting worse. It was no longer just interfering in her life; it seemed to be in control full-time. No other emotion had a voice. Everything in her life was now about anxiety.

As any good therapist would, I asked, "What about Sabre-Toothed tigers?" Our anxiety is meant to kick in when we are in danger. We cannot stop to contemplate the tiger in the rustling bushes. It is an instinctual response - *Danger! Run!* That is a pretty important response to keep. Our body gets all hyped up on endorphins and adrenalin so we can get to safety. Anxiety is different from stress, although they may have similar symptoms. Anxiety is fear-based. The problem with my client's anxiety is that it had lost perspective. It kept showing up and overreacting in situations that were not dangerous. It was out of control—overthinking, overanalyzing, keeping her awake or taking over dreams. She was curious about this idea of her anxiety being something that was meant to protect her. Even if she was pretty certain she was safe when it came to tigers in general.

Jack's Story

Jack was only a teenager when we met and expressed that he had no clue what anxiety even meant. He thought it was when you are worried about the future and explained that the future is exciting to a kid! The first time he felt anxiety in his body was during a basketball summer camp when he discovered he had lost his love for the game and did not want to continue. He felt anxious because he was unsure of the consequences of not participating. He says, "My heart rate increased, and I got anxious thinking about what I would have to face in the near future."

The next summer leading to junior high school, he experienced it again. "This felt different, like a weight on my chest and heavy breathing, and my heart racing." What is especially frustrating about anxiety is knowing that there is no danger or threat against you but still having these emotional reactions to ideas or events. For Jack, this general anxiety was developing into a set of compulsions that controlled the way he performed nearly every action. He counted the number of footsteps he took in sets of four and felt compelled to touch objects with both hands for an equal amount of time. He slept with his ears touching the pillow in the same position in a symmetrical way. These obsessive-compulsive experiences persisted for a few months before our first session.

We used the Empty Chair technique to learn more by giving his anxiety a voice. Jack talked to Anxiety who told him it was showing up to keep him safe. That made it much easier for him to interact with his anxiety empathetically, which helped him calm his nervous system and lessen his compulsive rituals. You cannot get rid of anxiety with rational thinking, it needs a voice. When Jack heard Anxiety say it was showing up to help, he began to cry. He said he did not realize Anxiety was coming to help him. With that perspective, I asked Jack how he could be more supportive of Anxiety. He thought maybe his anxiety would not show up so much if he could manage his fears.

Rather than focusing on the anxiety itself, the focus needed to be on how he could feel safe. Ways to quell our anxiety involve both the emotional part of our brain (often called the heart brain) and the rational brain (thinking brain). Experiencing moments of peace and calm can help us feel safe. There is no need for anxiety to show up when we feel safe. Breathing techniques can help by grounding us in the present moment and holding space for what is happening in our body. Typically, anxiety comes with accelerated breathing and an increased heart rate. Slowing the breath is a way of slowing the heart rate. It's as if Anxiety says to itself, "Huh, deep breaths, a slow heart rate. Everything must be cool here."

Exercise is good for moving the excess energy that comes with anxiety. Being in a fight/flight state generates a lot of energy that needs to go somewhere. Burning it off with exercise means it has somewhere to go. Otherwise the energy may manifest as racing thoughts or a set of compulsive behaviours, like it did for Jack. Before we begin looking for solutions, however, we need to start with recognizing Anxiety's pattern and how it is showing up in your life specifically.

- How does anxiety show up in your life?

- Which situations are ones in which anxiety feels compelled to take over?

- Can you identify the thoughts and feelings that accompany the anxiety?

- Where do you feel anxiety in your body? (Rather than jumping straight into exorcizing anxiety from your life, be a curious observer.)

Holding Space for Depression

"Depression is the flaw in love. To be creatures who love, we must be creatures who can despair at what we lose, and depression is the mechanism of that despair." These are the first two lines in Andrew Solomon's book, *The Noonday Demon: An Atlas of Depression*. I first encountered Andrew Solomon on a TED Talk where he speaks very candidly about his own experience with deep depression. The kind where he was lying in bed one day, knowing something was very wrong, but not being able to reach out for the phone to call for help. All of us have known melancholy. Perhaps some have had bouts of depression that are more of a dark night of the soul—that place of deep exploration of our self. That meaningful place in the world where we can experience the depth and richness of life because anything else feels damned pointless.

The American Psychiatric Association describes it this way, "Depression (major depressive disorder) is a common and serious medical illness that negatively affects how you feel, the way you think and how you act." You have a greater chance of experiencing depression if it runs in your family. Genetics is a major contributing factor as are environmental factors. If you are experiencing things in your environment you have not experienced before (poverty, bullying, retirement), they can trigger episodes of depression even if you have not experienced major depression before. Grief and loss often contain elements of depression, which left unchecked can lead to clinical depression.

The hardest part about depression is that these dark times in our lives do not necessarily keep the schedule you expect. Depression may show up out of the blue years after a trauma in your life. Holding space for depression is a way of cultivating a healing environment both in our external environment and our internal nervous system. It can be very confusing when it shows up as soon as life seems to be going well.

There was a time in my life where I identified with Solomon in that I knew there was something very wrong but I did not know what. My dark time of postpartum depression had me reaching out to my doctor describing what I was feeling as dissociative—it was as if I was watching my life in a movie. That scared me. Having a baby is a time we think we will be joyful. Depression feels incongruent, as if it does not belong. It can be incredibly difficult for someone experiencing a depressive episode to reach out for help. Especially if it is at a time when we think people will not understand or accept us.

Oftentimes, when we do reach out, we are met with simple suggestions "go for a walk" or "cut out gluten," which feels dismissive. Platitudes like "everything happens for a reason" or "that which doesn't kill us makes us stronger" may make the person experiencing the depression feel deficient. As if depression is a character flaw rather than a state of being; something you could avoid by being a better person. Healing from depression can be a long road for both the person experiencing depression and the people in their life who love them most. Helping a loved one feel that you want to be there can start with listening, as listening is not the same as problem-solving. "That sounds difficult." OR "I cannot imagine how you are feeling, but I want you to know I love you." This is what it means to hold space for the emotion.

Depression can leave a person feeling foggy and/or forgetful. The simplest things are difficult for a person experiencing depression, so offer (or ask people) to get groceries, cook meals, help with banking. Day-to-day tasks that provide support in a concrete way. Not only does this allow you to hold space for depression, it can help you feel helpful rather than helpless. If you notice changes or things that seem different or out of the ordinary, talk to your loved one. Let them know you are concerned and suggest they seek medical help. Perhaps offer to go with them or prepare a list of symptoms. Most importantly, be patient. It can take a long time for the person to get on the proper medication or see results with a therapist.

Holding Space for Sadness

In a world where everyone is chasing perfection, we can judge ourselves harshly when we struggle. As if struggling means you have done something wrong. However, we all struggle at some point. Life is difficult and not one of us will escape the pain that comes with walking through challenging life experiences. The biggest problem is that we think we need to struggle *alone*. The western culture of individualism measures our success on what we can do alone. And we compare ourselves to others: "She got over it, so should I" or "This person survived something far worse, so my suffering seems over-the-top." These thoughts are not focused on love and compassion.

Additionally, if a person shares their hurt, we tend to want to fix it. It feels good to solve problems. We are uncomfortable with messy feelings and situations so we look for order. Our world is a mess right now. It is why rates of anxiety, depression, and suicide are up. We do not exist to be happy or to make other people happy; we exist to love each other, right where we are. We can witness, acknowledge, and hold space for our emotions and states of being. But then, what if you want to move on from sadness?

Nicole's Story

Nicole's first question in therapy was frank, "Why am I so sad?" she demanded. Her son Elliott was just shy of his second birthday when he was diagnosed with acute lymphoblastic leukemia. He had what Nicole thought was the flu on-and-off for several months. Regular stuff that parents do not worry too much about–low energy, fever, night sweating, and loss of appetite. His parents asked for a specialist when Elliott had bruises that never seemed to go away, and nose bleeds every other day. No one expected the diagnosis Elliott's parents received that summer.

The next two years were taken over by hospital stays, chemotherapy, and constant reassurance to family and friends. There was very little time for anything else. Dad spent every moment he was not at work with his wife and son. Mom went into beast-mode: ensuring Elliott had the best care, the right pain management, and that any additional costs associated with his treatment were payable in manageable chunks. She did not want financial stress interfering with the time they needed to spend as a family.

When the dark times were over and 5-year-old Elliott was getting ready for big kid school, it seemed unbelievable. How could a child as sick as Elliott had been now be doing normal kid activities? Like *miracles*, the word *cured* seemed like one of those things you want to believe in but are unsure about. Nicole believed Elliott's situation was a miracle. It was during this first year of "normal" when Nicole began to experience depression. She describes it like a heavy blanket that enveloped her so that she could barely get out of bed.

When she did get out of bed, it was long enough to get Elliott off to school before seeking the comfort of her bed throughout the morning. What did she have to be depressed about? How could she take one day for granted wasting away in this sea of sadness after receiving a miracle? She could not even imagine the alternative story. Her self-loathing at her sadness seemed as heavy as the depression itself. The depression fed the guilt, and the guilt made her even more depressed.

Reaching out for help gave Nicole a perspective she had not considered. What if her depression was really recovery? She had spent over two years being a caregiver 24/7, not knowing what the outcome would be. Elliott had gotten used to getting his regular chemo treatments like he had his daily nap. It was a normal part of his routine. Nicole, on the other hand, had been through a traumatic experience, even if she didn't think of it like that. Cancer was happening to her son, not to her. She thought her sadness made her a horrible person.

In reality, she was a mom who had been through an unfathomable experience. Nicole needed space. It was going to take time to learn how to be a mom to a regular, healthy kid—a kid who needed to be reminded to do mundane tasks like pick up his toys and who needed to be disciplined. Understanding where her sadness was coming from was the first step in allowing and letting it take up some space so it could be witnessed and processed. She needed space for joy in her life too. It would take time for her to feel safe again experiencing that joy without looking over her shoulder for the dark cloud to her silver lining story.

Holding Space for Grief

Although every person experiences grief, what we consider "normal grief" is marked by movement towards accepting the loss. This can be complicated by circumstances, however. Grief can be complicated if a person experiences abbreviated grief by replacing the loss immediately with someone or something else. After losing one job, getting a new job may cut short the time you feel you can grieve. It can happen to children who lose parents if the other parent remarries quickly. If a person did a lot of grieving work anticipating the loss, then there may be an expectation that the grieving process has concluded with the loss itself.

In Nicole's case, her grief was complicated by feeling like she had nothing to grieve at all. During Elliott's treatments, she got to know many families that *didn't* get to bring their children home. She was experiencing disenfranchised grief. Her situation was one where there is no space for the grief to be acknowledged and validated. Grieving a child who *lived* does not seem like a normal thing to do. This also happens when people lose loved ones to dementia, mental illness, or substance abuse. Since the person didn't die, there is no room to grieve the loss of the person they were.

People who die through suicide, overdose, in drunk driving accidents, or from a disease considered high risk by society (e.g. AIDS) can leave survivors uncertain about how to hold space for the loss. The same may be said for people in same-sex relationships, families of gang members, or people who have lost their relationship to an extramarital affair. There is so much controversy around these types of losses that the griever may not know where to go with their feelings. Other people may find it hard to create space for their grief because they're mourning what society deems insignificant—the loss of an ex-spouse, colleague, a beloved pet, or the loss of a pregnancy, whether through abortion or miscarriage. Holding space for these feelings and actively working through grief is vital to the work of healing.

Without holding space for it, unresolved or masked grief may impair our day-to-day functioning, yet the person experiencing it may not recognize their symptoms as grieving. The inability to grieve over an extended period of time may eventually lead to physical symptoms as our nervous system works on overdrive to keep us regulated around the grief. That takes a lot of energy. Directing all our energy to keep our nervous system in balance can lead to our other systems (cardiac, respiratory, digestive, etc.) slowing down to conserve energy. Unprocessed grief can show up as an ulcer or chest pain—the result of our system not having the energy it needs to function properly. If we are not able to actively grieve, our nervous system will go into hyper-drive convincing the world around us that we are OK.

Grieving can be complicated when it is not fully acknowledged and expressed. Perhaps something is going on in your physical health or emotional life that does not have a clear reason. It may be time to consider whether or not it is unresolved grief due to a loss in your past. If it is, then it is time to hold space for that grief so it can be healed before it becomes chronic or exaggerated. Delayed grief needs a voice to heal, that is why it may crop up at odd times. Have you ever had an experience where things seemed to be going great in your life and then some issue from the past knocks on your door? It waits until it thinks you have time for it.

If you happen to work in a helping or healing profession (counsellors and therapists, rescue workers, police officers, doctors, and lawyers), you are at risk for vicarious grief and trauma from holding space for other people's emotions. Regular self-care may have been part of the training that you received in these professions, but if you're new to self-care, think on the following questions:

- How do you take care of yourself regularly?

- Do you check in with yourself or others to explore the possibility of unresolved grief and trauma?

- Do you create space away from co-workers with dramatic lives, people who ask too much of you, community tragedy, etc.?

- Do you set healthy boundaries with people who cause trauma in your life?

- Are you spending your time anticipating grief?

Scan your history for possible areas of secondary trauma and grief. You may not have been directly connected, but it may be something you still have to heal. Holding space for grief and trauma is the most important first step on the healing journey. We can look to our past experiences to see if there is anything there, but what if the experience has not happened yet?

It's important to also hold space for grief you are anticipating like a sick family member or an unexpected diagnosis. We live in a world where we are so interconnected that a situation doesn't need to be directly affecting us to cause us grief. However, it does mean the grief is ours and we need to hold space for it in our lives. You must resist the notion that you are not entitled to the grief you feel. If you feel it, it is yours to heal.

Nicole's grief came with a side-order of survivor's guilt. That can happen when someone survives a traumatic event when others have not. Why them and not me? Older people may think that as well, if they lose a child or grandchild. It does not feel like the natural order of things. Survivor's guilt can happen in accidents where someone dies while someone else survives. It does not make sense or seem fair, so we feel guilty. When it comes to grief, guilt is a distractor. If you did not intend to cause harm, there is no reason for guilt. What you probably feel is the overwhelming desire to have done something differently or wishing you had more time.

Nicole did begin to feel her sadness lift in time. She took medication for a few months, through the winter when she felt particularly low. It helped her turn on the lights so she could see the path beyond depression. In our work together, she was able to honour her depression as a gift. It was *not* something that showed up to rob her of joy. It was keeping her safe from breaking down completely. It was the stepping stone to her healing.

Nicole began feeling safe to tell her story—the fear she had when Elliott was first diagnosed, the energy it took to be positive through the most difficult experience of her life, the uncertainty of the future. Although she had appeared superhero strong, most of the time, she felt raw and vulnerable. By telling her story, she found some compassion for herself. And, she began to realize it is possible to hold two seemingly opposing emotions simultaneously. She felt grateful because her son had lived and sad because of everything she missed out on in the years consumed by cancer. Most importantly, she learned how to be a regular mom to a healthy kid.

REFLECTIVE ACTIVITY

Life Graph

Draw a straight line across the middle of a piece of paper and start with your earliest memory. Life Graphs represent the highs and lows of your life. The higher the point, the better the experience; the lower the point, the worse the experience. See if you can find at least 15 moments or events from your life that are important enough memories to include in your graph. As much as possible, include the month/year and age you were when you had this experience.

The Life Graph gives you an aerial view that may enable you to see patterns, clusters, themes. When you have finished the graph, go back and see if you can remember how you felt at the time or messages you received. Those messages may be part of the lens through which you see your story now. It gives you a chance to determine what you want to take with you in your future and what you want to put down.

An exercise like this can be difficult, especially if there is a particular cluster of time when you felt abandoned or alone. Be sure you have a safe person you can trust to talk through anything that pops up, needing to be processed. Recognizing our past patterns helps us understand how we have adapted to survive. It may make sense if you see that an addiction began after a particularly difficult time in your life. Perhaps it was how you coped. The part of you that thought the best thing to do was to numb the rest of you from the pain.

The idea with this exercise is to understand how the story of your life has unfolded. It may highlight unresolved emotions that could use some space. Once you see, you cannot un-see so be prepared to enter in to that space and allow the parts of your self that may be stuck in that part of your story to speak and be heard. That act alone is powerful in the healing process.

CHAPTER FOUR

LETTING

How to put down what is holding you back

"Surrender to what is.
Let go of what was.
Have faith in what will be."

Sonia Riccotti

Life is loss. When I studied transformational learning, I realized that we are learning and growing from our life experiences all the time. Yet, throughout my life, I had only learned to acquire things—career, home, partner—but not how to lose them. At the very least, I did not learn how to work through the grief that accompanies loss. Like everyone, I have had my share—loss of my dad through separation, then suicide; loss of jobs; loss of trust. The biggest losses for me came in 2002 when I lost my son Sam in January and then my daughter Tess in September. I was 20-weeks' pregnant with each one when they died. Even though I went on to have a baby the following year, I was torn between my sadness for the children I had lost and my joy for the child that I had.

Our culture does not leave a lot of room for this contradiction. Yet here I was feeling both sadness and joy—my heart was broken, yet my heart was full. In that experience, I realized that I could hold both of these conflicting emotions at the same time. Loss and struggle often allow us to take stock of what's most important in life. Journaling over the past 25 years has given me proof of how setting and reflecting on intentions has helped me manifest my life up to this point. It has also helped me endure the struggles that have come along the way. What I learned in my search for healing was the art of letting go—of my past, my anger, my hurt, my expectations, and, ultimately, of the weight that was a physical manifestation of my emotional pain. It all felt so heavy, and it was time to lay it down.

You have to let go of some things to make room for new things. It was time to let go of some emotional pain and make room for my grief. In the last chapter, we talked about holding space for grief. However, grieving and mourning are something active that you do. One of our most difficult life lessons comes when we realize we have not been taught *how* to lose things, including people and pets. Grief may also result from losing someone or something you did not get a chance to love. For example, perhaps you were estranged from a parent—when they die, you lose them, but you also lose any chance of reconciliation. It can make grief complicated. You could end up feeling disenfranchised, as if you should not be grieving because you did not love the person deeply.

Grief does not only include the loss itself, but all the hopes and dreams you may have had for that person or thing. There was a whole future you may have anticipated, which leaves missing pages in your story. How you thought the chapters of your life would unfold needs to be rethought or reordered. This is not part of grief work in our culture. There is a tendency to push ourselves and others forward, our eyes set on our goals for the future.

Life is lived by considering all aspects—our past, present, and future. When we experience loss, it feels overwhelming. Our past wants us to hang out in the memories, which is painful. Our present wants us to experience and process the pain. (Yikes!) So, often, our future wins. We busy ourselves reordering our life, being pragmatic and getting on with it, while leaving our past and present parts of self abandoned in the process.

Consider the life graph you just completed. Are there places where you may have moved too quickly? Situations you lived through but did not consider from various perspectives? Once you recognize the full impact of these events on your life and who you are now, the easier it is to identify the stories that need to be processed so you can lay them to rest. Letting go is not about burying things and leaving them behind. It is about integrating parts of the story so it is more cohesive.

HEALING FROM LOSS

Letting go can be freeing, whether it is an old gaming system gathering dust in your basement or an old grudge that has been taking up space in your heart. After holding on to them for many years, I recently decided it was time to burn some of my old journals from a period in my life that was particularly difficult. I no longer wanted a reminder of the struggle because I felt I had acquired the lesson of healing. The point of my writing was not so much about insight into the struggle but a way to intentionally search for meaning. I write to find the lessons that I know are there if I look for them, so I can choose to leave behind the struggles and carry forth the lessons. That is the power of intention; I should plan (hope for the future) and reflect (learn from the past), but the most important thing is to make room for today. These are the lessons we learn in our struggle and grief.

Grief is learning to take things one step at a time. Through my studies and my own life experience, I have learned how to take those steps, and feel called to share the lessons I have learned as a therapist, speaker, and writer but also as a friend, wife, and mother. If you did the reflective activity in the last chapter (Life Graph), go back to it and see if you can identify the lessons you learned through those experiences. It can be an important step to understanding ourselves if we can find meaning in our experiences. This is different than the platitude *everything happens for a reason*. Having free will means that other people's decisions and choices in life may hurt us. The process of going back through our story to find meaning in the experience helps acknowledge the events in our life had an effect on us so we can experience and process the feelings and emotions, take what we need, and then put the rest down.

Resist the urge to get stuck in a story trying to figure it out or obsessing about avoiding that same experience in the future. The point of engaging in reflective exercises is to witness and let go. We keep the lesson. Perhaps we can identify where we have built resilience. Our authentic self is the witness for everything that we experience, including our thoughts and emotions. It is our awareness—the subjective "I". The quicker we can learn to bring ourselves back to our authentic self during a challenging situation, the easier it is to release the hold these stories have over our lives.

Experts believe that the reason we have memory is for the evolution of our species. Our memory and imagination parts of the brain are in close proximity. What that means is how we interpret the memories from our past experiences can influence how we imagine our future. If our story has been one of pain, we may only be able to imagine pain in the future. A client with a string of bad breakups may say that she is the constant in those stories. That means she can only expect the same story over and over. But what if she looks at those relationships as a witness? Finding compassion for the part of herself that experienced the pain can help her shift the story.

In quantum physics, we know that the act of observing particles changes them. It was a fascinating discovery scientists made during their experiments. Particles would behave one way in an experiment when left alone but then a completely different way if the scientist was observing. The very act of observing becomes a variable in the environment, which affects the outcome! This idea of the Observer Effect has since been expanded to other fields of study like psychology and sociology. Imagine what it would mean in our lives if the mere act of observing our story were to shift it. I am contending that it does. By going back over old stories or witnessing past thoughts and emotions in the present, we can change the outcome. It is in the future where we may be able to see and measure changes more concretely.

Ken Wilbur says, "...awareness in and of itself is curative." Looking for meaning in our stories is one way to shift because we are transformed when we look for learning opportunities in our experiences. You could be a whole new person just by reading this book and considering new perspectives from the experiences you've had. The act of witnessing our emotions means they have been processed and can be released. We have now allowed them to pass through us. Imagine that the reflective act itself changes our story in the past too. Where before it was one of pain and loss, it now becomes one of resilience and courage.

As the universe expands, so do we. We are in a perpetual state of motion. Emotion simply means *in-motion*, so we must allow our emotions to move. As they move through us and we experience them, we change. Pain is often our resistance to that change. Fear of that pain may keep us from doing healing work. We may find ourselves in a state of anxiety, not wanting to experience the pain of hard situations and circumstances. We may work hard to push unpleasant emotions down by distracting our minds with other things in life. What is our fear? Perhaps it's that we will be lost in a sea of emotion if we allow our feelings in. Once you realize you are not the emotion itself, but rather the "I" experiencing the emotion, you may be less resistant to it.

No one likes to feel pain. But letting it wash over you can be cleansing. Having a good cry can be like that. We may not like it as it's happening and may go out of our way to avoid it, yet allowing it can leave us feeling lighter. The key is to understand that you are no more the feeling you are experiencing in your heart than you are the chair that is holding your body. They are separate. Each of us experiences thousands of thoughts and emotions each moment. Why do we cling to some and let others flow through us? Many times, it has to do with the way we have experienced this emotion in the past.

We have two types of memory. The first is explicit and includes both semantic memory (general knowledge, facts and figures) and episodic memory (recollection of personal experiences and events). Our episodic memory also includes our *interpretation* of events and experiences. We decide how to store the memory based on the meaning we have given the event. Think about episodic memories like sections of a library. We may store our memories of bad breakups under the general heading "Relationships". Now, whenever we think about developing a new relation- ship, our brain runs to our library and pulls the stories we have stored in it. If we have decided relationships and bad breakups are the same thing, our brain will run back with the evidence we have sent it to find. We may use that evidence to support our view that if I look for a new relationship, it will end in a bad breakup. To let go of that view, we need to look at it through a different lens. Maybe the real issue is the choice of partner. Perhaps a person's values did not align with ours. Looking for lessons and meaning in our experiences means we can re-categorize our memories and use them as evidence for something that supports our goals and dreams. We can move these old stories into different sections of our mind's library.

The second type of memory we have is implicit memory. This type is also divided into two areas—procedural and emotional. These are the memories that are part of our subconscious. Procedural memory is why people say, "It's like learning to ride a bike." Once you learn, you can access that learning through muscle memory. You no longer have to think about what you need your body to do. You just ride! Emotional memory works the same way. What happens is that you attach the emotions you felt during your experience to the experience itself. Maybe there is a relationship loss in your Life Graph. Allowing yourself to experience the unresolved emotion (sadness, anger, disappointment) can help to separate the feelings from the experience. In that way, you can learn from the experience and store it as something that will serve your growth rather than have each encounter with a new relationship trigger your emotional memory from your past experience.

HEALING EMOTIONAL PAIN

Imagine free-falling a thousand feet. No one would expect you to heal from that kind of injury in a couple of weeks or even a couple of months. There would be setting bones, surgeries, and rehabilitation. You might not ever be the same, but you would heal. It's the same with a broken heart. One of the myths of grief is time heals all wounds. It doesn't. Time is a necessary component of the healing process, however.

Healing is hard work, whether it is physical or emotional. Trust the voice of exhaustion—it knows when you need to rest and recover. You also need support as you let go and heal from old emotional injuries. Don't be afraid to reach out and ask for it. There are people who will love you right where you are and stick with you as you recover. Working in grief and trauma has taught me a few things about letting go and healing from the emotional pain that may be keeping you from thriving in your life.

Everyone Heals Differently

There is no magic healing formula for healing. Imagine you experience a big loss in your life, and I say, "OK, the depth of your attachment x length of time you had this relationship divided by your age = 44 days of grieving." As crazy as that sounds, that's what often happens with our expectations around healing from emotional pain. Have you ever heard someone say, "They should be over it by now!" about a friend or colleague? I hear that a lot in therapy. People come because they wonder if they should *still* be grieving after a certain amount of time. Perhaps they are judging themselves or feeling judged by others.

Relationships are complex. Sometimes they are complicated. There may be regret, things you need to forgive or apologize for. There may be things you wish you could go back and say. It takes a while to work through that stuff, so take your time and do it in your own way. There is no medal for the fastest griever. There is no such thing as emotionally healed. **We heal.** Healing is a process the same as any other system in our body. Just as our digestive system processes food, our nervous system processes emotions. Others will want to give advice or share their stories along the way. You can consider it all, but in the end, you have to trust yourself and your own healing journey. Grief does not understand time. It understands healing. Your healing will be as unique as your loss.

Grief Comes in Waves

If grief came all at once, you might drown. I think stretching out our grief is a way of protecting ourselves. I call it *layered grief*. It's the same grief, but with a new layer. Grief ebbs and flows throughout our life. It does not mean healing is impossible; it just means it may be part of your new normal—an ache from an old injury. Yes, we are healing. We just have times when our heart remembers it has been injured. I had a client who lost both her parents within a week of one another—one expected, one sudden. She was grieving and healing, beginning to experience happy moments here and there without feeling guilty. Then, her daughter got engaged. The grief that accompanied her happiness for her daughter was unexpected. She realized that every family event without her parents would be difficult. Same old grief but with a new layer. Knowing that grief may be a part of your future experiences can help you find a place for it.

Grief Accompanies Many Forms of Loss

When we think about grief, we often assume it is connected to the loss of a person, but all change includes some form of loss. When your child goes to school, you may grieve the loss of the toddler you were raising. They are the same person, and yet they are different. When I look back at pictures of my kids, I miss those versions of them dearly. I love the people they are today, but my heart aches a little too.

Divorce is a transition that can come with feelings of grief as well. Even if you both agreed, it's still a loss. You may grieve what you could have had or what you did have when you started your relationship. Whenever you go through a change—moving, losing your job, getting married, having a baby, graduating—try to leave some room for grief. Grief doesn't necessarily mean you're unhappy about the change. It just means you feel sad as you let go. Allow yourself time to take what you need to learn from the experience, about yourself and about life, then you'll find that you can move.

Hope is Part of the Healing Process

Hope is knowing that somehow, someway, you will make it through. It is impossible to imagine ever moving through the heavy fog of grief in the immediate aftermath of a loss. Hope can help us put one foot in front of the other even when the world is spinning. When you lose someone close to you or experience a big life change, it can feel as if you have lost yourself as well.

When one of my clients lost her mom, she worried that she would not like the new person she would become as a result of the loss. At times, she grieved as much for her old self as she did for her mother. When some of those parts of herself began to re-emerge a year later, she was relieved. It was like encountering an old and trusted friend. She was eager to integrate these parts with her new self, who she thought of as wise, having gone through something so difficult. When you cannot imagine ever feeling anything but sorrow, hope can help us hold many emotions at the same time—trusting they are all there to support us on our healing journey.

TELLING STORIES OF LOSS

Joan's Story

"He was just a dog!" she said. The tears that threatened to spill down her face said otherwise.

"He was your friend for 18 years", I replied.

"But Barb in Accounting lost her mom last year. How can I take time off to grieve for my dog when she didn't take any time for her mom?"

Being raised in a culture that encourages competition, we tend to compare everything. So, Joan was faced with a dilemma—give in to societal pressure of "move on" or give in to her heart. Joan sought counselling to help her manage through the pressure of this decision. Perhaps she would find strategies for coping with the stress. The fact that I was a grief therapist came as a surprise. When I said it might be a meaningful coincidence, she agreed. "Do people really come to grief counselling when they lose a pet?" she asked. People seek healing from all types of loss. Every relationship has a story. Stories need to be told.

Joan's dad had brought this particular dog home just 6-months after Joan lost her mom to cancer. According to her Dad, his official name was Rusty Ol' Bag of Bones. Even at 10, Joan knew that was no name for a dog. Rusty had been there for Joan through everything. A single constant in a life of transitions—teenage years (including teenage heartbreak), dad's remarriage, moving away to college (close enough to come home on weekends for Rusty). At 28, Joan had never been in the world as an adult without her best friend. She had no idea how she would manage without his unconditional love and acceptance.

If you've ever had a pet, you probably know the kind of love I'm talking about. It is different from people love. Pets are completely dependent on us, like children. Unlike our kids though, they never stop needing our attention. Have you ever had a relationship with an animal? They seem to take on our characteristics. Or maybe they are more like our alter egos.

We can pour much of ourselves, our lives into these relationships. And often, they teach us as much as we teach them.

Joan taught Rusty to fetch and stay by spending time in the yard. He taught her patience by eating her shoes and slippers. She taught him not to bark at strangers. He taught her the value of being a good listener. Joan poured her grief onto Rusty when she lost her mom. She trusted him with her insecurity and doubt. She talked through all major decisions with him. Even though he did not talk back, the act of talking it through out loud helped Joan make decisions. It helped put the possibilities or steps into a linear sequence, which helped her feel more confident about her decisions.

Joan and I worked through the grief recovery process just as I would with any client who lost someone significant. Many times, grief work includes other areas of loss. Joan had lost her mom, her sense of security, and some of her childhood around the same time she had gotten Rusty. Children tend to grow up fast when they lose a parent. Joan was trying to manage through a story that her friends did not understand. Losing Rusty brought back some of that grief. Joan recognized that grieving her mom as a 10-year old child was not the same as grieving her mom as a 28-year old woman. She still had some stuff.

Letting go means processing our emotional pain. Part of grief recovery is about challenging the assumptions of grief and what it means to grieve. People may not understand your grief regardless of who or what you have lost. It is about looking at ways we have coped with loss in the past and deciding if coping methods are harmful or helpful. Joan and I looked at the ways Rusty had supported her and where she might get that support now, through her grief. We examined some of the typical yet unhelpful sayings we hear about grief, like "Be Strong," and found more helpful sayings. "Be Real" was one Joan liked. Especially for times when she heard that voice in her head pushing her to move on when she did not feel ready.

In the end, Joan did not feel her relationship with Rusty was incomplete. She realized she had mentally prepared for this loss as he aged. She felt she had been as faithful to their friendship as he had. Where she did feel things were incomplete was with her mom. There were a lot of things left unsaid in that relationship. Just like the Life Graph, we were able to graph out her relationship with her mom and look for emotions that felt unprocessed and things she didn't get a chance to say.

Part of my training in the Grief Recovery Method[1] includes writing a letter to the person you've lost so you can say the things you may not have had a chance to say. It is similar to an Empty Chair exercise—you can apologize to them for things you did (or didn't do) and forgive them for things they may have apologized for if given more time. Of course, some relationships are complicated and need a little more therapeutic support, as in cases of abuse and trauma.

HONOURING THE LETTING GO PROCESS

"Grief is a normal and natural reaction to loss", says John James, co-author of the Grief Recovery Method. It is also as unique as the relationship itself. There are no phases, stages, or steps. Even if you have had a loss in your life before, each loss demands something different. Think about your healing from the perspective of mind, body, spirit. Do something that engages the mind, like journaling. Also, do things that give the mind a break, like yoga. Personally, I cannot think and do anything physical. I have to focus on the moves or I may get injured. It's a nice break for my mind.

Grief can leave you feeling physically, as well as emotionally, exhausted so it helps to find activities that produce energy (walk in nature) and ones that conserve energy (an afternoon of getting cozy and reading). That is healing for the body. Rituals and ceremonies can help honour the spirit. Joan bought a special memorable box for some of Rusty's special toys, photos, etc. You can paint a rock for your garden, write a poem. Something that honours your memories in some way. Healing takes time and intention.

Regularly remind yourself that what you are doing is part of the healing process. Part of the process will include figuring out who you are now— you *after* loss. Love changes us, and so does loss. Be gentle with yourself.

---

1   The Grief Recovery Method is a step-by-step guide that promotes recovery from grief. Many have been trained and certified in this method and use it as part of a comprehensive healing strategy. Readers can move through the process themselves, however. For more information, visit their website griefrecoverymethod.com.

Have you ever tried to hold back tears? It can take a lot of energy. You hold them back because the thought of letting them out means you might drown in them. Tears need a voice as part of the healing story. Whether they are sad tears, tears of frustration or righteous anger, they need to be shed to do their job. They help our body let go of the stress the situation we've experienced has produced.

I remember the first time I read the book *Yesterday, I Cried,* by Iyanla Vanzant. Her story, and the poem by the same name, are about the day she cried for all the things she needed to cry about but never did. It made me cry too. I cried for her. And then I cried for myself. I wrote my own version of my story based on her poem. Like her, I ugly cried those snottin' and bawlin' tears. Do you know which ones I mean? The kind of crying tears that make your whole body shake and heave with the heaviness of the story. I also cried those soft weepy tears of compassion for the parts of me who lived through the story. Tears are useful in washing away pain. Why do we dishonour them by rushing them out or pushing them down? Do we see them as a sign of weakness? Well, they're not. They're necessary. Their job is to help us heal and our job is to let them.

Iyanla's story is one about a woman who was broken—and then broken open by crying for herself and being a witness to her story. I learned what it meant to cry with an agenda—to tell my story and cry to heal it; to let myself go, and let the tears cleanse me. If we do not shed the tears, they cloud our judgement. We will end up stuck in the same story over and over but with different characters. We become loyal to patterns and themes in our lives that are familiar. We relive the same story until we get the lesson that will allow us to move on to the next chapter.

Look at your life story and really observe it. Each time you live through an experience, even if it feels like the same experience over and over, you have the opportunity to learn. Resilience is like a muscle. When we work out, our muscles tear. It is in the recovery where they become stronger. You may find that each iteration of what seems to be the same old story gives you a chance to learn at a deeper level. Until you get the lesson you need, you may find you have the same experience over and over.

As Iyanla held space for her story, she learned how to fall apart and keep moving forward. We never stop. There is always something to heal, something to learn, someone to love. That is life. It is perpetual motion.

We can let it happen to us, or we can jump into it and navigate it towards something amazing. We do not need to stay stuck. But, if we want to move forward, we must process. We must engage with the pain, cry the tears and let them carry us to the next level.

Every challenge we face offers us a chance to reflect and learn. Reflection helps us make decisions that can bring about the future we envision for ourselves. By allowing our emotions to process through us, we guard against losing our self in the process of healing. Life is messy and complex. The way to healing is to let go of how you *think* life should be and get on with leaning into how it actually is.

We know change is inevitable, yet we get stuck in our ways, and the status quo seems the easiest path. Status quo and fulfilling other people's expectations for our life may feel stable in a busy world. Our nervous system loves that. Staying still is very safe! We set goals and get caught up in striving, yet we may constantly feel as if we are falling short. As if there is a busload full of people who know exactly how to move through life while we ride the short bus. We are travelling together on our earth path; yet, we often think we are the only one.

Thriving is just as much about being authentic in the present as it is setting goals for the future. We are going to mess it up; we are going to hold on too long to things that no longer serve us. We are going to doubt ourselves and our decisions. We may feel guilty about the things we did or should have done. We may feel shame that these thoughts and feelings point to character flaws. All of us hurt. All of us carry a backpack of pain. How would your life be different if you could figure out how to put some of it down?

Change *is* inevitable. It is up to us to decide what it will look like and who we will be when it's over. Life can be messy and uncomfortable, and we've already decided we don't like to experience pain. We prefer to medicate; to "get back to normal", as the Tylenol commercial encourages us to do. Life is unpredictable and uncertain, so our goal should be to learn how to relax into it. Experience it as it comes and let go of anything that is unnecessary for our journey.

THE ART OF FORGIVENESS

Children get into scuffles, hit one another or call names. Parents intervene and insist the offender apologizes. We're taught to say, "I'm sorry." It is our parents' way of teaching boundaries and good manners. Insisting children apologize when they do not mean it, or when they do not understand the transgression, may not be helpful, however. The same can be said for the victims, as they may not want to accept the apology by shaking hands or hugging. The whole thing can easily erode into a set of socially acceptable boxes we check to re-establish equilibrium. Children learn they need to move through a system and may miss the deeper point of forgiving and apologizing. As an adult, that training can leave us confused on the whole issue of forgiveness.

Psychologists define forgiveness as something a person does consciously and deliberately to release feelings of resentment. Forgiving someone does not mean you condone the offence or accept an excuse. It does not necessarily mean you continue to have a relationship. It is something you do more for yourself than the other person. It is possible to forgive someone even if they are not part of the forgiveness process. To forgive means putting down the weight of the situation. It is meant to bring you peace of mind. It is said that people who are hurting, hurt people. Empathizing with another person's journey and how they may have gotten to the place where they hurt you can be a way to wade into forgiveness. Forgiveness is you saying, "I understand what led you to this place. What you did was not okay. But I understand."

It is often the case that people who treat others in an uncaring or cavalier manner have experienced the same treatment themselves. Being able to forgive may be easier if we consider that *our* behaviour has probably negatively affected others in some way. We may not even be aware of how we have hurt another person. If we consider forgiveness and apology together, it may give us a new appreciation of how to forgive. We live in a flawed world. We all hurt people unknowingly.

- Who do I need to forgive?

- Who needs to hear an apology from me?

- Are there places in my life where I am holding resentment?

- Am I *thinking* more about how I feel than actually *feeling* the emotion? (Moving from your head to your heart is part of the healing process.)

Sarah's Story

Sarah had a difficult childhood. Her father was an alcoholic and when Sarah was only eight years old, he began treating her in a sexual way. Sarah identified her childhood wounds as the source of her current unhappiness and thought talking it through with a therapist would help. She had successfully incorporated a mindful yoga practice into her life but felt there were old wounds that continued to cause her pain. She was looking to put those old stories down and heal those wounds once and for all.

Her grief therapy included writing a letter to her dad. In it, she told him that his alcoholism and inappropriate sexual behaviour was messed up and he should have had more control. He was a dad and should have protected her, not hurt her. She was so angry with him! She wrote that even though his choices were not okay, she realized he also grew up with a violent alcoholic father. Although Sarah did not know much of her father's story, she empathized with the little boy who must have felt as scared as she did.

Sarah took the opportunity in the letter to apologize to her dad for not letting him know how much she appreciated the financial support he provided for her education. It helped so much, and she was not sure he ever knew how grateful she was for that support.

In her letter, she told her dad that she would be putting down her story of "abused child" and focusing instead on healing her wounds. Becoming a mom gave her the opportunity to break the cycle of abuse and focus on living playfully, joyfully. She would love her own inner child the way she deserved to be loved and treated as a little girl. She would no longer re-read or re-tell her old story.

Sarah did not give the letter to her dad. He died a few years back. But the letter was not for him anyway. It was for Sarah. When she read it to me, there were a lot of tears. Her tears were ones of purpose and intention rather than tears of sadness. Cleansing tears. Afterwards, she felt lighter and eventually left counselling with hope (and a plan) for her healing.

"Forgiveness is an action, not a feeling." That comes from the Grief Recovery Handbook too. The method encourages grievers to take steps towards healing one-at-a-time. Stop reading for a moment. Take a deep breath. Search your heart. Is there a heaviness of hurt? Is there a burden you have been carrying that you want to put down? Forgiveness puts you in charge. It allows you to take back your power, which is often the first step towards healing. The experiences you had become a chapter, but they are not the whole story. You get to pick up the pen to write and rewrite the story of your life.

REFLECTIVE ACTIVITY

PART 1: *Progressive Relaxation*

Letting go of emotional pain means tapping into the subconscious mind where it may live. Thinking about healing from emotional pain is different from *experiencing and letting go* of that pain. For this reflective activity, I want you to put yourself into a deep state of relaxation. Start by doing a progressive relaxation exercise. Settle yourself in a seated position or lay down flat. Uncross your arms and legs and take a deep breath. Imagine that each breath takes you deeper and deeper into a state of serenity.

See if you can use your breath to locate any pain, stress, tension, or trauma in your body. Start at your feet and begin breathing into different parts of your body. On the inhale, locate the tension. On the exhale, allow your breath to take it all away, so there is room for peace and comfort.

Take at least 10 minutes to use your breath to bring you into a state of relaxation. If your mind wanders, bring it back to exercise. You may find it helpful to narrate the activity in your mind so that you are listening to your own voice in your head walk you through the breathing steps.

Being in a deep state of relaxation can feel like that space between wakefulness and sleep. I describe it like floating in water—you may be aware of the world around you, but you are contained in your own experience. You can hear your breath. It is as if you are experiencing the world from the inside. You may want to practice Part 1 a few times to see if you can achieve this state of relaxation. Once your mind and body are completely relaxed, it is easier to access the subconscious. What that means is you will move from the part of your brain that wants to rationalize and problem-solve and into the creative part where imagination lives.

As you do Part 2, be open to images that may appear. The things that live in the implicit, emotional memory may be a new way of experiencing for you[2].

---

2   If you have experiences of trauma in your past, I encourage you to only do this second visualization with a therapist who is trauma-informed and/or someone skilled in Internal Family Systems (IFS) Therapy. Having someone who is trained in traumatic memory is key to helping you make sense of the images.

REFLECTIVE ACTIVITY

PART 2: *Whole Self Healing*

Once you have found that place of relaxation, imagine you are going on a journey of self-discovery. That journey will take you to a place of healing and recovery. It is an opportunity to feel whole. A person who is becoming stronger and wiser as you improve your understanding of life and your purpose of living.

Imagine you are walking towards a room. In that room are all the parts of your personality—the helpers, the healers, the rebels. There may also be emotions (like my angry part) that show up. The parts may be different ages—young, inner child parts; teenage parts, young adults.

You smile. You know these parts. Now, imagine opening the door and sitting at the head of the table. These parts of your personality have come to the table to listen to you. Even the reluctant ones have shown up with the hope that things can feel more balanced. That they may be able to connect to a shared purpose.

Even though there are many parts to your personality, imagine them working in harmony. See which parts of yourself show up—young parts, hurt parts, parts that you want to control. Some show up excitedly, some reluctantly. Some may want to sabotage (that is a pretty common trauma response). As you visualize yourself meeting these parts, imagine them working together so that all the parts move together as one. All the parts moving together towards a shared vision. Set that vision in this place of relaxation and imagine how it feels to be on that journey. It's about the process as much as the destination.

Before you begin, take a cleansing breath. Smile at the group. Let them know you come with a solution, that you have decided to live a life of contentment and fulfillment and purpose. And that you need their help. Many hands make light work, you tell them. You are a team. Working together with mutual respect and love, you are much more likely to achieve your goal. Imagine the parts signing a contract agreeing to follow you on your journey towards growth and healing. Perhaps the contract is a handshake or a hug. Something to acknowledge agreement. Let the reluctant parts know you'll stick with them until trust comes.

Your joy in achieving this harmony within yourself outweighs everything else. Even in the face of an occasional setback, which is inevitable, you continue to move forward together. Each setback can be experienced as an isolated incident. Perhaps a lesson. It does not mean the collapse of what you are building long-term. It is only a small interruption.

You have the capacity to visualize yourself in the future now. Living up to your dreams with a sense of joy and fulfillment. Know that your unconscious mind and the centre core will continue to guide the process like an internal coach. Every moment of the day, through the weeks and months to come. Until you are travelling easily together.

CHAPTER FIVE

HEALING

How to program your nervous system for success

"God whispers to us in our pleasures, speaks in our conscience, but shouts in our pain."

C. S. Lewis

Trigger Warning. Although I talk about trauma throughout the book, this chapter dives a little deeper into it so make sure you have a safe person you can reach out to if you feel triggered or dysregulated. Regularly check in with your nervous system as you read to ensure you feel safe.

With divorce rates over fifty percent, sexual abuse at 1-in-4 for women and 1-in-8 to 10 for men), war, violence, addiction, pandemics—it would be a miracle if you didn't have some kind of trauma wound. We all have a story. Those stories include hurt, pain, and loss. Unless we can face those unpleasant parts of our past, it's all but impossible to find the hope we need to thrive in life. Engaging with our stories may feel terrifying. In this chapter, we will explore how to do that while staying grounded in the present moment.

We have talked about the need to ground ourselves in our values. My guess is that healing is one of those values for you, which is why you reached for this book. We must heal our trauma in order to live our lives inspired and with purpose. Unresolved trauma is the thing that keeps us stuck—a barrier to living our best life. Healing may be the very thing that can open the door to finding joy.

In earlier chapters, we found our way to mindfulness. It is the awareness that comes from an observer's mind or wise mind. As we explore what it means to heal trauma, mindfulness will help us tune in to the sensations in our bodies. Before you read any further, take a deep breath. See if you can locate any nervousness, apprehension, or fear. We are not trying to get rid of them, just notice them. By noticing, you remind yourself that you are the awareness of the feeling, not the feeling itself. Allow the emotion, but be sure to check in with yourself periodically to see if your body is sending you signals that you have had enough for today. If that is the case, you can continue the work of healing trauma by putting down the book and spending time in your body. Move around, take a shower, breathe.

The goal in trauma healing is to stay connected to your body, so you learn its unique language. It sends you signals for healing and safety constantly. We have been trained to tune them out. This chapter is about learning to tune back in, find ways to settle into a place of peace and calm internally, regardless of what is happening in our external world.

TRAUMA IS A WOUND

While most of us think of trauma as an event, trauma is actually a wound. Regardless of the event itself, if it has led to repressing memories or emotions and has taken us off course from the person we were becoming, the event has wounded us. Trauma is the wound or scar the event caused in us. Physical trauma results in physical wounds, like broken bones. Even if they are healed, you can see where the wound was. Emotional wounds are harder to see but they are the result of circumstances that have left us feeling anxious and afraid or angry and closed off.

We know that people who experience extreme circumstances are at risk for post-traumatic stress disorder. PTSD is our own memory trapped in the emotion of the experience. It can affect the episodic memory by making the sequence of events fragmented and difficult to remember. The memory may be spotty, but the pain is intensely real. PTSD does not feel like a memory but rather feels as if you are reliving the event again and again. That's because traumatic memory is processed differently than other memories.

By looking at trauma as an event, it is easy to put it on a sliding scale— this trauma experience is worse than that other one. Referring to it as capital "T" trauma and small "t" trauma does the same thing. Think about a physical wound from a car accident. If you arrive in the Emergency Department after having been in a car accident, the doctor will not ask if it was a capital "C" car accident or a small "c" car accident. They are going to assess and treat the wounds. A decent physician would never look at the accident and say your injuries are incongruent with the event. "It was a fender bender for crying out loud; don't you think a broken femur is a bit much!" Yet, we do this all the time with emotional wounds.

In his book, *The Body Keeps The Score*, Bessel van der Kolk tells us that "...trauma is not just an event that took place sometime in the past; it is also the imprint left by the experience on the mind, brain, and body. Trauma results in a fundamental reorganization of the way the mind and brain manage perceptions." If you are interested in the science around trauma and how the body processes it, I encourage you to read his work. It is very comprehensive and spans his whole career as a physician working with trauma wounds in patients. He opens up a new understanding of trauma and the wounds that come from the experience.

What happens in our brain as the result of trauma is that our brain now perceives everything as a threat. Imagine being in a constant state of hyper-alertness. Being in that state makes it impossible to ebb and flow through life's experiences. Our system is now either in a state of hyper-arousal (anxiety) or crashing into hypo-arousal (depression). Our goal in healing trauma is to open the window wide so we can live our lives day-to-day without anxiety and depression trying to help keep us safe. It is learning to settle the nervous system so that we are resilient to change and can accept loss. Not only are we able to recognize and understand our feelings, but we are also able to actually *feel* our feelings. Feeling them is how we process them and let them go. It takes us from feeling over-whelmed, which may garner a fight/flight/freeze response, to a place of settling.

Polyvagal Theory is Stephen Porges' work around how the sympa-thetic and parasympathetic nervous system work to keep us emotionally regulated. When there is trauma, all the energy goes into keeping us safe from the threat that we perceive all the time. That sounds exhausting, doesn't it? Most of us have some trauma wound from our past experi-ences. By dismissing them as small "t" trauma, we cannot fully process the emotional pain caused by the event, which means we cannot fully heal. We never fully regulate our system so that we can experience life as it comes—allowing it to pass through our awareness but not settle in and take up the space we need to live on purpose.

When people say, "Everything happens for a reason", I know it is their way of trying to make sense of a tragedy or give comfort to others. But what reason could there possibly be for some of the senseless tragedy that happens around us? This saying implies there is some external force sending tragedy our way in an effort to control our lives and that we have no control over what is happening in our world. The truth is many of the tragedies that happen in the world are a direct result of the choices people make. That is the reason: cause and effect. Conditions culminate, something happens, and life unfolds in a way that we were not expecting.

Every one of us has probably experienced this at one point or another in life—experiencing something where we did not have any control of the outcome. However, we *do* have control over how we react to the situa-tion. We *do* have control over what meaning we take from the experience. Of course, that doesn't necessarily tackle the question: *why*? Why did this happen to me? In 1981, Robert Kushner published *When Bad Things Happen to Good People* as a way of trying to make sense of the tragedy of losing his young teenage son. It was his attempt at answering the *why* question. Why do children die instead of growing old? This was Kushner's struggle in his writing. We all struggle with questions of why.

For me, one of the most difficult questions I face is, "Why does someone take their own life?" It is a struggle for anyone who has experienced loss from suicide. The only way I can wrap my head around the kind of struggle that results in suicide is to imagine the person swimming. They seem to be okay, or maybe they struggle a bit, but then they keep swimming along with the rest of us. You may notice them struggling a lot. You may see them looking for help or holding on to a life preserver (a friend, a routine, a memory, a purpose). You may even offer support. Sometimes the world weighs too heavily, and they simply go under. That may happen a few times. Someone may throw them a rope, but they are too tired to swim for it. The journey is too long or too difficult and the struggle feels unbearable. At some point, they just let go.

There are others struggling who we don't notice at all. The struggle is beneath the surface. They float along like a duck—smooth and calm on the surface, paddling like hell under the water. They may not even realize how hard they are working—those are the ones whose deaths surprises us. Letting go may be just as surprising to them as it is to us, in fact.

People leave. Business deals fall apart. Bullies are everywhere. These events are a part of everyday life; however, they can leave behind emotional wounds that change how we experience the world forever afterward. During the struggle, clients have told me, "I want the pain to stop. I want the struggle to end. But I don't want to die." The first time someone said that to me, I jolted. I had not considered that a person who dies from suicide (which I now call dying from anxiety, depression, trauma, grief, etc.) might not have wanted to die at all. They simply wanted the pain to stop. They may have used up all the energy necessary to keep swimming and then just let go.

My clinical diagnosis on suicide as a response to difficult life experiences is that it sucks. You may have been expecting a more sophisticated analysis from me, but this is where I land on it. It sucks that we live in a world that is so painful for some people that they can no longer live in it. I want to honour the memory of all those who have died by creating a world of love and connection. There should be pockets of space where a person can float and gather strength, so they can continue to swim with the rest of us. I want to be someone's soft place to fall. We can change the world by seeing one another, *really seeing*. Not through the lens of ego and status. Seeing someone with our glasses off—the good, the bad, the ugly—and loving them anyway.

Most of us have been taught to cope with difficulties in life with our rational minds. "Be strong" or "time heals" or "they're in a better place."

People may be well-meaning, but the messages we get around loss and struggle are not always helpful. Yes, your loved one may be in a better place, depending on belief, but you're not! Healing traumatic wounds is not a rational act. It is the work of the heart—sharing stories, developing rituals, and holding space for your tears, your anger, and even your gratitude. Knowing all that, today, I still grapple with *why* when it comes to some tragedy.

We live in a world of systems—families, schools, communities. Our past experiences within these systems develop our meaning schemes. These meaning perspectives are the filters through which we view the present – I am strong/I am weak; I am smart/I am stupid; I can do this/I cannot do that; I feel hopeful/I feel hopeless. Our meaning perspectives shape how we live our lives, the choices we make, the relationships we have. Ultimately, they shape what we believe about ourselves and our futures.

Trauma makes it difficult to put the chapters of our story into a coherent sequence so we can learn from it. The trauma story does not have a beginning, middle, and end as most stories do. So, we fill in the gaps. It's our rational brain's attempt to make sense of things that don't make sense. We like a complete story. If we do not have a clear understanding of how our past experiences have shaped our understanding of the world, we cannot make meaningful change in our present lives.

People who feel as if they have little control over the outcome can develop an underlying feeling of hopelessness; a sense that things have always been this way and are bound to stay the same. *This is a dangerous place to live.* This view of the world as unsafe is a lens through which present-day events are judged. By challenging our meaning schemes, we can tell a different story. We can look through a different lens—a lens where we have compassion for ourselves and hope for our future. Although I might say I am a resilient and hopeful person by nature, there have been times in my life when I have felt overwhelmed. As the "strong one", my pain is often invisible to those around me. *Strong* is the mask I wear. My mask is like a cast on an emotional wound. What wounds does your mask cover?

Things become complicated when our grief and trauma overwhelm us to the point of feeling powerless. This feeling of powerlessness can make a person feel very vulnerable. We may feel helpless to find a way forward. This loss of control over personal circumstances produces a sense that things are bound to stay the same. It feels like swimming against a strong current. Even though you may be an experienced swimmer, there are times when the circumstances surrounding you feel overwhelming. You may have experienced strong currents or undertows before and have managed to keep swimming. But this time feels different. You feel as if you are drowning. This is when some people will call out for help—they will talk to a friend, see their doctor, see a counsellor, all in an effort to keep going. Some will need to tread water for a time to gather the strength they need. For some, the current comes on too fast, or they are treading water too long. They begin to feel helpless. And hopeless.

LEARNED HOPEFULNESS

Martin Seligman and other positive psychologists believe that not only are we meant to repair the worst in life, we are also charged with building on positive elements. Just as we can learn to be helpless and hopeless from our experiences, we can also learn to be hopeful. Learned hopefulness comes from drawing strength from our experiences. It builds on the theory of self-efficacy—your belief in your ability to learn new things and integrate new skills into your life. Resilience comes from believing in yourself and your ability to survive difficult circumstances. You build on the experiences where you learned new skills that impacted your life positively. As you do, you become more confident and develop a sense of control to change your life. You develop hope by continuously building upon your stories of strength and resilience.

A study done in 2009 shows that positive psychology interventions significantly enhance well-being and decrease depressive symptoms. In fact, they found that behaviours like engaging in enjoyable activities, using one's signature strengths, using cognitive strategies (replaying positive experiences and self-monitoring instances of well-being), and engaging in the practice of mindfulness can all have a positive impact on one's psychological health. Surrounding yourself with people who inspire hope and support healing is key.

Much of the literature today around trauma focuses on the mind-body connection. We experience emotions in our body, but western culture pushes us to live more in our rational mind, as if thinking is superior to feeling. Many clients who come to therapy are able to describe how they feel from an understanding point of view. Few are comfortable actually feeling the emotion. If someone tells me about an experience in their childhood that had a huge impact on their life, I will ask them where they feel that sensation (say sadness) in their body. That question often brings a deer-in-the-headlights look. We are simply not taught how to feel our feelings in our bodies. Rather, we encourage children *not* to feel. Kids are great at allowing emotional outbursts. We train them to control their feelings. We have all become so good at controlling our feelings that we forget how to process them at all. Where do you think all that emotional energy goes?

Stress is a state the body experiences when directing all its energy towards trying *not* to feel. Our autonomic nervous system has three states that determine our sense of safety. The first is secure and connected. If our experiences are ones where people responded to our needs, then our nervous system is regulated, and all our other systems work without issue. If it were a traffic light, this is green. All systems go. However, if we feel threatened, our system takes us into a state of hyper-arousal (fight/flight). It's when the light turns yellow. If we can make it through this state safely, we can return back to green. If not, the light is red. Stop! This means our system goes into a state of hypo-arousal (freeze/collapse), and we go offline.

The root of most traumatic wounds are experiences where we felt immobilized. Think about times in your life when that may have been the case. All the times when you may have felt powerless in situations and circumstances. Acknowledging that we have traumatic wounds is the first step to healing them. The next step is understanding how we have adapted to cope with our hurts in the past. We adapt to survive. It is the thing that serves us. If you had parents who fought or were not emotionally present, you might have adapted to the family story by ignoring the problem, even if your body had been signaling to you that you were unsafe. The core fear for children is abandonment.

When you feel insecure, it will manifest in patterns of attachment called *Anxious* or *Avoidant*. Anxious children are the ones with the big emotions like crying, yelling, clinging. They look for safety through the story "If I'm big, they won't leave." As an adult, you may experience anxious attachment whenever you feel threatened. It looks like a constant need for reassurance from others or a strong desire to be in control. Anxious, insecure attachment makes us strive for perfection. As in, "If I'm good, they won't leave" and relies heavily on other people to help us feel emotionally regulated.

Another child in the same circumstances may have adapted as Avoidant. They look for safety through the story "If I'm small, they won't leave." Those are the children who are quiet, keep to themselves. We may label them as deep, thinkers, soulful. They are loners. Although these are legitimate character traits, for a child who has experienced trauma, it can be an adaptation. As they grow, the avoidant insecure attachment may look like social isolation.

As an adult who shifts into avoidant behaviour when I feel threatened or insecure, it can look like me wanting to squirrel away by myself with my journal and a cup of tea, figuring myself out before re-entering the real world. Avoidant people rely completely on themselves for emotional regulation because trust is an issue. It can be difficult for people with avoidant patterns to be vulnerable.

Some people have *Disorganized Attachment* patterns. They tend to move back and forth between Anxious and Avoidant. That adaptation is more common for people who grew up in an environment that was unpredictable. One day my parent is calm and safe, the next they are raging and dangerous. As adults, the pattern may manifest cycles of attachment then detachment. Today I am all in. Tomorrow I am out of here! They learn to be agile so they can respond to the circumstances. That may make it difficult to commit to anything—a university major, a career, a partner. If they are married, they may only feel comfortable putting one foot in. The other is ready to run if things go sideways. Disorganized patterns of attachment can be confusing for their partners.

Although we may have adaptations for times when we feel threatened or insecure, we may also have experiences with secure attachment. Secure attachment looks like trusting yourself and your environment. We are more in the ebb-and-flow of life and have a wide berth for difficult circumstances. Secure attachment means we are able to return to a state of emotional regulation quickly. We can make meaning from our situations and take lessons that lead us to be more resilient in the world. Most people have experienced secure attachment in some form, just as we have all experienced periods of insecurity. Understanding our adaptations helps us set up our environment so that we stay in a state of emotional regulation and secure attachment.

To complicate matters a little further, we can have different attachment styles to different people, places, and things. For example, I may feel securely attached in my relationship with my grandmother but have an anxious response to an overbearing boss. My visit with her leaves me feeling light and loved; my meeting with him leaves me doing what I call the Dancing Bear—internally and unconsciously asking myself what can I do so he will appreciate and value me. (That part of me is very young.)

Sometimes these adaptations can seem incongruent. If I have a secure attachment to God, who I believe will provide all things, how can I have an anxious attachment to money? Our relationship with food can be disorganized in a diet-obsessed culture. Eating can give us a sense of control, which makes us feel secure. Weight can be a barrier to our goals and dreams making us feel insecure—eating chips every night wondering why we are gaining weight is Avoidant. Calorie counting, hours of exercise, weighing ourselves daily (constantly measuring our inputs and outputs) is Anxious. So very disorganized.

- How did patterns of secure and insecure attachment show up in your childhood story?

- Where do these patterns show up for you now – relationships, career, finances, health?

- Which patterns need healing?

- What emotions do you need to befriend? (Emotional regulation means allowing and witnessing for the parts of yourself that may not have had a voice in the past.)

- Who can you reach out to now for connection and safety?

Rita's Story

It started in childhood. Just like how an infectious disease can weaken the immune system, Rita experienced poverty in her childhood and it weakened her sense of security. There were times when there simply was not enough; she remembers being hungry. It was not the norm, but it left her hypersensitive to situations of scarcity. Rita had an emotional reaction of anger every time her mother mentioned being financially strapped—an environmental trigger that transports her back in time to a different story. Rita's mother worked hard throughout her life, but she had never made a great amount of money. Any money she did have, she would give to anyone who needed it more than she did. The anger Rita felt whenever the subject of money arose was her own money insecurity.

Although she had a good job, her money psychology was one of scarcity. Under the anger was fear—what if there is not enough! Rita would be angry and then immediately feel shame. She would spend a lot of time beating herself up for being mean or cold towards her mom. These were self-imposed labels she could not seem to shake. Finally, she began to examine the trigger. Looking at her feelings as separate from her, Rita imagined herself having relationships with these feelings.

If we choose to let them in, we need to be prepared for what they have to say. Like an old friend coming to visit, they may come with baggage—stuff you may need to examine using mindfulness or Empty Chair. If we deny, resist, and ignore difficult emotions, they may come rushing in, overwhelming us and leaving us feeling helpless. They may become an unruly guest or overstay their welcome. Those require much more attention. It's best to give them a voice before they take over our life and our health.

OPENING THE WINDOW

Dan Siegel came up with this visual of a window to show what happens to our brain and body after an adverse situation. When the nervous system is healthy, there is an up-and-down flow. Something happens, we are triggered, we go up or down, and then we settle back to calm. Stress on the system can cause the window to close, however. It becomes smaller, which means it is easier to move into states of heightened or lowered arousal. Hyper-arousal is excessive energy that feels like anxiety, fear, panic, or overwhelm. Hypo-arousal is shutting down, the feeling of going numb, or freezing. Our autonomic nervous system reaction is to return to a state of calm.

Our system has the ability to self-regulate like any other system in our body. The problem arises when our system is overloaded. Being in a constant state of stress makes healing trauma impossible. We want to control what is happening in our external world, but our coping strategies often come with guilt, shame, and judgment. Perhaps because they are not optimal for our overall well-being—overeating, drinking, medicating, sleeping, gaming, or binge-watching all six seasons of your favourite show in a single weekend. These can all make us feel calm in the moment, but coping in this way is not so great long-term. To complicate it, we tend to focus on our reaction as a character flaw rather than seeing it as an attempt to self-regulate, which leads to more shame and guilt and judgment.

What we really need to do is recognize what is happening, rather than judging ourselves, and figure out how to shift back to healthy functioning so that we are not in these extreme states. Being able to identify what is happening in the moment—*I am in a state of dysregulation*—is the first step to recognizing what it is. Then, we may be able to identify what the emotion causing our dysregulation is, based on where we feel it in our body. Once we identify it and become aware of it, we can give it a voice.

We can waste a lot of time trying to control thoughts or feelings, which is nearly impossible. It is much easier to come up with ways to process them when they do appear. Better yet, we can spend our time doing things that will keep us ebbing and flowing within this window of tolerance, so we don't feel ourselves peaking and crashing in states of hyper- and hypo-arousal. Rather than spending all your energy trying to manage symptoms, decide to put that energy into maintaining an internal healing environment.

Healing trauma is twofold: telling our story is a chance to make connections and find meaning. We can look back and see where we have adapted. We can let go and change the story. Changing our relationship to our past can change our future. The data you store around memory can now serve your imagination. If our story was "nothing ever works out for me", confirmation bias would ensure that nothing ever does. Every time we encounter difficulty, our brains fetch the message that it won't work out. Healing the story means bringing in another possibility.

The second way we heal trauma is in the day-to-day awareness of what is happening in our emotional life. It is incredibly important to move from judging ourselves for our reactions to compassionate curiosity: "How do I feel? What was the trigger? What am I feeling in my body?" Physical ailments manifest from emotional stress. The point is that we all have complex emotions, and sometimes those emotions are triggered by our environment or past experience with attachment and security. We have to understand what is happening and then find things that support us thriving in the chaos of a world in perpetual motion. Committing to healing means emotional regulation, which in turn will lessen the peaking and crashing states and move us into ebbing and flowing. How do we do that? Daily practice.

The Vagus nerve, which is the principal component of the parasympathetic nervous system and responsible for our emotional regulation, is composed of 80% afferent (body) and 20% efferent (brain) fibres. And the movement is up from the body to the brain, rather than the other way around. Think about the last time you felt nervous. Where did it start? Most of us would describe it as butterflies in our stomach. When we feel sadness, it may be a heaviness in our chest or constriction in our throat. We feel it in our body before it even registers in our brain what is happening. Instead of sticking with it, taking deep breaths and processing the feeling, we go straight to our head to analyze and solve the problem. If the problem is in our body, the solution is *not* in our heads. It is in our bodies.

The way to stay emotionally regulated in a chaotic world is to find ways of being calm and settled in our body regardless of external circumstance. Being able to keep that feeling of calm when recalling difficult memories, and finding ways to connect with other people through difficult circumstances are key. We are social creatures. We need to talk about the things we are experiencing and witness for one another. We can honour what we did to survive. It was an adaptive response that we created to keep ourselves safe. Once we acknowledge it, we can let it go and do something different.

Oftentimes, the ways of being in the world that helped us survive hold us back when we want to thrive. We need to learn to scan our bodies to process the emotions as they come up rather than looking to our brains for an answer. Emotions reside in our throat (lump), chest (tightness), or gut (butterflies), or some other part of the body. Our feelings do not need a complicated explanation. There is a big difference between looking for the reason why you need a hug (rational) and being hugged (emotional). Feelings need to be felt. They need us to let them in and experience them regardless of the cause. These feelings have shown up for your attention.

If we see our mental and emotional injuries like physical injuries, our healing may look similar as well. We would assess and treat the wound itself, rather than determining the state of what the injury *should* look like based on the event. Our healing patterns may follow the same course—ICU when the injury is debilitating, a hospital stay when you need ongoing care, and finally, time spent in rehabilitation before determining what life looks like after the injury. Moving forward can be hard work, take a long time, and be messy at times. New situations and circumstances can trigger a feeling of being unsafe—vulnerable, like a small child. Fear can hit you at the gut-level and you can feel yourself shaking from the inside out.

If you have a chronic physical injury, it may ache when the weather turns damp. We don't tend to judge that physical response, it's just how it is. We learn to care for it. We have to learn to do the same with an emotional injury. What are the situations and circumstances that have brought you back to this old wound? How is it the same and how is it different from the original event? Understanding the phases of trauma recovery helps us work through the healing process as soon as a trauma injury has occurred.

HEALING RECOVERY

Healing can be an elusive term. It sounds like something we want to do, but unlike physical healing, which sometimes takes care of itself, emotional healing requires us to work with it. The good news is that once we learn how to set our system up to deal with daily stress, it will work as passively as our digestive system. Alex Howard, a trauma practitioner in the UK, uses the analogy of digesting trauma through emotional regulation just like we digest food through our system. If emotion is like food, reflecting is like chewing. We need some time to break things down. Swallowing breaks it down further—allowing and letting the feelings process (tears, anger, delight). Energy is created when we metabolize food, just as insights and revelations happen when we metabolize emotional responses. The last thing we do is expel or get rid of anything that we have not absorbed. In the same way, there are things that each of us carries from our past and things people in our everyday life want to push on us. Letting go and putting it down with intention is an act of releasing what does not serve us. Processing emotions takes a body, mind, spirit approach for optimal healing.

Connecting with your <u>Body</u>: Nervous System Regulation

Emotional regulation requires emotional safety. To quickly establish safety, you need to connect physically to your body.

- **Give yourself a hug**. Wrap your arms around yourself and squeeze. Putting pressure on your body will help you reconnect to it. Weighted blankets help too.

- **Shake it out**. Have you ever seen animals fight? Once it's over, they shake or flap their wings. They are letting go of the excess energy. You can do that too. Shake your arms. Shake your legs. Go for a walk, run, swim. Move your body.

- **Breathe**. Use your breath to slow things down and get yourself back into a place where you can think. The method does not matter. Just breathe. For example: breathe in for 4 seconds, hold for 4 seconds, breathe out for 4 seconds. Then move up to 5 seconds each, and then 6 seconds each.

Connecting with your <u>Mind</u>: Becoming Aware

- Being able to quickly understand and adapt to what is happening in the moment is how to heal the trauma every day. **Acknowledge, witness, validate, heal.**

- **Be present**. It is easy to jump to judgment. What you really need is compassion. These parts of yourself need understanding and love. If you find the judgmental feelings pushing their way in, say "stop" or "not now."

- **Find your voice**. It may be important for you to have a conversation with someone safe about how you are feeling. You may need to tell your story again. Or, you may want to tell it for the first time. It can be empowering to say it out loud and have a witness.

- **Recovery time is key.** You may feel like you need a day off. Your energy may be low, or you may want to be alone. Allow yourself to check in with that wise part of yourself. Trust your instinct. The world will not end if you take a sick day.

Connecting with your Spirit: Integrating the Story

- **Emotional trauma from past events.** These experiences can cause the protector part of your self to over-develop. Schwartz tells us that some parts of our self needed to be strengthened in our past to protect us—these are the managers, protectors, firefighters. They are dominant as a way of keeping us safe in a dangerous or emotional situation, we exile the parts of our self that were vulnerable—playful, curious, carefree. Integration is the key to working from your spiritual self—the part that leads the whole system to move in harmony. Healing is the work of the soul.

- **Trauma is only part of the story**. This thing that happened to you? It is not the whole story. The part of your self that experienced the trauma may have a loud voice in your life. But, there is also a part of you that wants to heal. That part needs a stronger role in your ongoing story.

- **Post-Traumatic Growth**. You may need time to reconnect to your present-day self. This is where your resilience can be cultivated and strengthened. The part that sees itself as strong and capable. It is important to remember how much you have learned and grown from your experience. *Be Strong* is not something you do. It is who you are.

Experiencing a traumatic, emotional wound can lead us to wonder who we are or who we should be, or would have become, if we had not experienced the event that led to the wound. Who we may have become is a loss. You may feel sad. You may feel ripped off and have some righteous anger. Give those feelings some space. They deserve it. The road to recovery can be long but worth it. Stay the course. Healing means continuing to put one foot in front of the other. You are the person you are today based on *everything* that happened to you. So am I. I am grateful for my healing journey. I hope you are too.

WHAT I KNOW FOR SURE

In *Man's Search for Meaning*, Viktor Frankl concludes that life never ceases to have meaning, even in suffering and death—that the meaning of life is found in every moment of living. I believe that everything that happens to us is an opportunity to learn. That is how we thrive. We can judge our experiences as positive or negative, but either way, they are opportunities to grow, to heal, to challenge our old ways of thinking, to reach out, to stretch beyond our comfort zone. Ultimately, it is our choice.

In really challenging circumstances, when I have felt alone and abandoned, I search hard for the lesson. One day I realized—that is the lesson! Not knowing, being unsure, but continuing to have faith in life and the healing process. In the moment, I may not know the big picture. In fact, I may never know why this has happened to me, but I do know that I can choose to heal and have faith in myself. Faith that I will figure out how to keep moving forward and that I will heal. Perhaps I will be stronger for having gone through the experience. Maybe not right away, but somewhere on my life's journey. To me, that is the meaning of hope.

Our choice can come by not fighting against healing any longer. It is in opening our hearts and allowing ourselves to embrace life as it is in *this* moment. And, it is in being there for each other in our respective journeys that gives me hope for humanity. Life is complex and often complicated. Regardless of what shows up, feel it fully—appreciating the authenticity of everything that comes and grappling with our own struggles can open us up to the struggles of other people. Human connection is the whole point of life. We are all looking for the light at the end of the tunnel. Let's travel the journey together so none of us gets lost in the darkness.

REFLECTIVE ACTIVITY
Activate Your Healing Potential

To create a healing environment, pick one thing in each of these two states listed below (healing anxious states and healing avoidant states) to help your emotional healing. If there are things in these lists that you do already—great! Now, do them with intention. These are concrete, measurable things you can do to heal your nervous system and expand your window of tolerance. That expansion allows for more calm, peace, and serenity.

Healing Hyper-arousal or Anxious States
Decreasing Energy

- Rhythmic, deep breathing (slow heart, slow mind)
- Yoga – something slow, controlled (Hatha, Vinyasa)
- Calm music, humming, a weighted blanket at night
- Running or physical activity to burn off the excess energy (Ashtanga Yoga)
- Blasts of cold water at the end of a shower
- Connecting with someone safe and calm

Healing Hypo-arousal or Depressive/Avoidant States
Increasing Energy

- Body movement that gathers energy – dancing, rocking, bouncing
- Essential oils or burning incense – using the sense of smell to stimulate (citrus smells are good)
- Playing or listening to music – using your sense of hearing – again, humming or singing
- Doing anything creative – painting, crafting, writing

- Connecting with someone who brings the energy and excitement

Each time you engage in this action, you tell yourself: "I am in a state of healing." Check in with yourself at the end of the week to see if you have shifted your nervous system into a state of calm. These are things we need to do each day to keep our system healthy.

One kale smoothie is not going to do it.

CHAPTER SIX

DEFINING

How to create a world of love and connection

---

*"Not all of us can do great things. But we can do
small things with great love."*

Mother Theresa

What word do you associate with Warren Buffett? Wealthy? Rich, pros-
perous, billionaire or some such synonym? Perhaps it is words associated
with wealth like success, business owner, investor. Did you even once think
love? That is precisely what he said to the students at Georgia Tech when
they asked him about success. At the age of 90, being the third richest
person in the world, Buffett said, "The ultimate measure of success is not
wealth but whether or not you are loved." That's the ultimate test of how
you have lived your life.

The trouble with love is that you cannot buy it. You can buy things that
bring temporary pleasure, but the only way to get love is to be lovable.
That may be the biggest letdown for people who spend their lives in
pursuit of money. We would like to think that we could write a check for

anything we need if we could: "I'll buy a million dollars' worth of love." But it doesn't work that way. The more you give love away, the more you get.

Small gestures of love make a huge impact, like a drop in the ocean that creates a ripple. Each wave makes another wave spreading outward. Things like:

- Paying for the person behind you in the drive-thru.

- Helping a neighbour with yard work.

- Returning your neighbours' trash or compost bins (after the truck has been by, of course).

- Preparing and delivering a meal for a family dealing with a sickness, new addition to the family, or losing a loved one.

- Going shopping for someone who is unable.

- Delivering coffee or cold drinks to construction workers.

- Providing free babysitting for a single parent.

- Picking up trash on the street in your neighbourhood.

- Dropping a gift card to a person who regularly serves you.

- Sending an unexpected note of encouragement through email. Better yet, send it in the mail!

- Delivering some baked goods to a new neighbour.

- Being creative. Coming up with ideas of love to share.

Every major religion has a message for how to love. My experience is from a Christian perspective. However, while reading other faith perspectives, I found two things that seem to cross lines and show up in them all—one is suffering, the other is love. When asked by the officials about the most important commandments of God, Jesus said there are two. (1) Love God and (2) Love your neighbour as yourself. Think about the power of that in relation to our world today. Perhaps the problem is not that we do not love our neighbour, but that we do not love ourselves. If we love our neighbour as we love our self, but we do not love ourselves, what are we spreading? Judgement? We can be so hard on ourselves.

We have a chance to change the narrative. If the standard we hold ourselves to is one of love, how do you measure up? If success is love, how are you doing? The Ojibway People have a saying, "No tree has branches so foolish as to fight among themselves." We are all part of the same tree—the tree of life. The tree is a metaphor, meaning we are all one. If you find it hard to love yourself, love someone else. If it is true that we are one, loving your neighbour is an act of loving yourself.

LOVE YOURSELF

We all have voices we hear as the various parts of our self try to be heard. Perhaps it's a part of us that is younger, triggering us back to a difficult time in our life; or an emotional part (like anger) that overwhelms us. These voices are part of our consciousness. Understanding ourselves comes from understanding these various parts. By getting to know these parts better it can help us find love and compassion for ourselves. Unless we understand where these parts of ourselves are coming from, we tend to judge them harshly. For example, imagine you are cut off in traffic and experience road rage. You find yourself cursing and yelling at the person in front of you. That's not a typical reaction for you so, rather than dismissing the anger as an over-reaction and feeling ashamed, it can be helpful to find out more about that part of you that experienced the situation. Perhaps it is rooted in another experience in traffic where carelessness resulted in an accident. Perhaps it is a feeling of being invisible or taken advantage of in other areas of your life.

The jump to self-judgment may come from a time when you were unable to feel big or have "negative" feelings. Of course, it can help to have people in your life who see you for who you are and appreciate your gifts. We do not always see it in ourselves. There is so much noise. Sometimes that noise comes from other parts of our life and sometimes it comes from messages we receive from others. Taking the time to dissect situations and thinking about the various parts of self expands self-awareness and opens us up to self-understanding and compassion for times in our life that have been difficult and need healing.

Much of the noise we encounter today is on social media. Here is a pro tip on quieting the noise quickly and easily: **Never listen to the trolls**

on social media! They are nameless, faceless predators who aim to hurt. It is not personal. Their venom is about them, not you. This negativity and judgment can distort self-awareness. Social media began as a way for friends to connect to one another. It really was personal. It has grown into a system that is far from what it was originally. Although we may go on social media to connect, the entity itself has a dark side. It can be a place of judgment and competition.

Contrary to the saying, "A picture is worth a thousand words", it is not always the case when it comes to the photos people post online. Not many people post photographs of the giant fight they had right before the beautiful snapshot that tells the world "my life is awesome". Alternatively, and perhaps as dangerous, is oversharing on social media so that our personal stories of pain and trauma become a free-for-all of feedback and advice that can leave even the strongest person feeling unsupported and alone.

Our real friends, our people, can look right into us and say, "You got this. You are amazing. You are doing fine." This feedback, from the people that know all the good, the bad, and the ugly parts of our lives, brings a perspective that is difficult to attain on a social media platform. Most of us can easily find compassion for a friend, yet it's harder to do for ourselves. This is why the parts of self work is so important for healing. It is easier to relate to those parts as separate and find compassion as you would for a friend.

Differentiating the voices we often hear in our heads can help us find perspective, so that we know what things to consider more deeply and what things are not meant for our healing. If you encounter a persistent or particularly loud voice, ask yourself:

- Where is this voice coming from?

- Did I hear this growing up?

- Whose voice is this?

- Is this some invisible societal standard I'm trying to measure up to?

- What does the evidence say about how I'm doing?

Linda's Story

As a little girl, Linda was diligent with her dolls. Every morning she made sure they were settled while she was away at school. When she returned, Linda would make sure they were changed, fed, cuddled. She read to them and sang them songs as if these dolls were her first babies. As a teenager, Linda could be counted on at family functions to take care of the little ones. She would organize games, make sure they had snacks, and navigate through any mishaps that are inevitable with children. She was sought after as the neighbourhood babysitter—children would ask for her specifically. No matter what else she did in her life, Linda wanted to be a mother.

She got married at 26 and had her first son at 28. Ben was born prematurely with a few complications. He was fragile coming home from the hospital, and it was the first time Linda ever doubted her ability to care for a baby. Caring for a premature newborn took a lot of work, and Linda was exhausted most days. She wondered why she was not happy about becoming a mom when it had been her dream for so long. Doubt can be infectious. It began to wind its way around Linda's daily routine. Nothing she did seemed to be good enough. "Am I capable of being a good mother?" she wondered. These voices of harsh judgement seem to be saying the same thing to all of us:

- Why are you struggling when everyone else seems to get it?

- Why did you say that—are you stupid or something?

- Just *stop it* already (insert destructive coping behaviour here)

Going through her Life Graph, Linda began to see a pattern emerge. Her mom could never seem to do anything right in the eyes of her own mother, Linda's maternal grandmother. "The meal is not salty enough (or too salty)." "What kind of housewife gets a dishwasher or a microwave?" and "Men will wander if you are not trim." Linda realized her obsession with her dolls was practice for being the perfect mother. Obviously, her own mom could not teach her anything, according to her grandmother. Understanding and finding compassion for her mom helped Linda find compassion for herself. Upon reflection, she realized how helpful her mom had been the first year after Ben was born. She had a quiet confidence about her ability to support Linda that Linda had not noticed. Where did *that* come from?

I encouraged Linda to work through some of her self-doubts by talking more honestly with her mom. She learned a lot about the family dynamics and where some of the stories originated. With that, Linda was able to identify the voice more easily when it spoke. She learned to quiet it with practice, and objectively speaking, she was coping well. She was proud of her son's development and was able to find compassion for herself as a mother. When the voice of doubt crept in, she said out loud to herself, "That's not mine." It was easier for Linda to sort through what *she* needed to work on and what was part of her upbringing.

You may have to have difficult conversations with people in your life who dump their stuff on you by setting boundaries. Their advice or comments may come from a time in their own life they have not examined or healed. You cannot heal someone else's wounds. Notice if the voice you hear is not your own. Perhaps it is from someone who dumped on you, like it was for Linda. If what you are working through is not your stuff, give it back. Gently but firmly, letting them know, "That's not mine."

WHAT IS MINE?

One of my favourite shows growing up was *This Old House*. Remember that one? I had a Tuesday night ritual that included settling in with my specialty coffee and watching Bob Villa and Norm, the carpenter, as they brought a house back to life. It was not the home improvement show you see today on *HGTV*. Each house was a season rather than an hour-long episode. It took time. It seems to be the expectation in our culture today to do everything fast. We want things to be completed in the length of one show—start to finish; neat and tidy. However, some projects are more complicated and take time; they need care. This may be the biggest problem today when it comes to mental health. We are an instant results society. The focus tends to be on self-improvement, like the fixer-upper shows we watch. But what if mental health is less *HGTV* and more *This Old House*? What if we started thinking about our health from the point of view of restoration?

It is often the foundation that determines the extent of the project when it comes to the house. It has to be solid. In our lives, our foundation is our childhood. In adult life, it may require caring for our inner child, if we experienced trauma or insecure attachment. If you have stuff there, you may need to steady the foundation. That may look like patching or it could be a total rebuild, depending on your circumstances. That's why I love the term "good bones". No matter how bad a shape the place is in, good bones mean hope. The house may have been neglected, but good bones mean it held up anyway. It shows resilience, and it can be restored to its original state.

Regardless of our upbringing (our foundation), I believe resilience is something we can build upon. It is our inner strength with everything else built around it. When we think about our health, it is often from a self-improvement model. Self-improvement can mean glossing over the major things and going straight for the glam. It looks good on the outside, but the inside may not be strong. Have you ever had to spend a lot of money on a home project that was not visible? Think upgrading the sewer system. That is about as far away from sexy as a project can get. But no amount of painting or new trim work will make as big an impact on the quality of the property.

Our mental health is like that. It's less "exciting beach vacation photos on your Instagram" and more "30-days in rehab or weekly AA or WW". It is the private stuff we do to repair the foundation and structure that makes the most difference. The issue with having so much emphasis on social media these days is that it focuses on the least important piece—how things look on the outside. One of the things I loved most about *This Old House* was how long they spent on loving the house back to its original splendour. When it comes to our own health and restoration, I wonder how things might be if we focused less on aesthetics and more on structure and character. Restoration means stripping things down to the studs rather than simply adding things on.

If you took the time to assess, what would your foundation look like? Does it have cracks, or does the whole thing need to be poured again? There is a lot of inner child work that can help lay a new foundation for you to build upon. What about your structure? Do you have good bones or, as my grandfather would say, "Are you 'good people'?" Does your outward appearance fit with the state of the other two? Our health is about more than just the state of our mind. It includes all three – mind, body, spirit. What we may consider the rational mind, emotional mind (body sensations), and wise mind. Perhaps it is time to explore and take a season for yourself to do the work you need to do.

Our world moves so fast it is easy for things to fall into a state of disrepair. Our healing work is in inspecting the foundation by doing trauma and inner child work, shoring up the structure by living a principle-based life, and updating the aesthetics to fit how you want to feel in the world rather than measuring up to society's standard of beauty. Aesthetics may be physical fitness to feel strong and balanced. That can spill over into mental and emotional strength. Take your time. Restoration is a labour of love. Love yourself back to health.

LOVING OTHERS

Have you ever met someone and felt you knew them instantly? There is an instant familiarity with them. You feel comfortable immediately. It is as if you say, "Nice to meet you. I missed you." These are people that make you feel as if you are connected on a whole other level. I call these soul friends.

Namaste is what you say at the end of yoga or group meditation. It is my heart seeing your heart—free of judgment or ego. It is timeless so that you almost don't even have to say the word. The gesture of a smile or nod implies you are seeing the other person at a deep level. People long to be seen. In a fast world, where busy equals productive, the individual can feel invisible. Have you ever met someone who is surrounded by people daily and feels lonely? Has that person ever been you? Even if people are *namasting* all over the place, it does not necessarily mean you will feel connected.

That is why soul friends are so important. You are seen even though you may not say anything. My soul knows your soul; we are connected. Lucky for us, these friends can come in a variety of flavours. You may have many of these or a select few experiences. Regardless of the types of friendships you have experienced, the point is that friendships are an essential way to give and receive love.

Childhood Friendships

Who was your best friend as a kid? Most of us had at least one. Our relationships in childhood prepare us for a more complex world. We learn to build trust, resolve conflict, express emotion. Play is something that has all but been forgotten in today's world. Children are so scheduled with organized activities they may miss the benefits of developing relationships. Social media is a new way of connecting to friends when you are young. It is awesome for connecting quickly and often. It can broaden your social circle and make it easier for shy children to connect. Connection releases oxytocin, which is stress-reducing. The drawback when it is not a face-to-face connection is that the nuances of body language are lost. If someone is experiencing sadness or grief, you cannot hug them. (Hug emojis are not the same.)

Women's Friendships

Traditionally, women have been the keepers of relationships. Bonds are more likely to grow in these environments. Women will often seek one another out in times of stress. Women also tend to be stronger in communication, which makes it easier to talk and connect. And, it is not unusual for women friends to touch, hug, or braid one another's hair, making it easier to develop intimate friendships. In Victorian times, women had a lot of their love needs met through their relationships with other women. There were a lot of rules for courting and marriage so women's friendships became a safe place to explore love, even romantic love. (This may be why a lot of poems, flowery prose, and romantic novels emerged from this time period.) The same can be said for cultures that are touch-based—women touch to connect and feel safe.

Although modern times may make it difficult, women still have opportunities to meet friends through work, networking events, kids and playdates. These are great places to find those friends or acquaintances who become part of the going-out-with-the-girls group. It may be different nowadays as we expect to have many more of our love needs met in partnerships rather than friendships. Still, these types of friends can be so healing and encouraging, if you can find a good one.

Men's Friendships

In general, men lean towards compartmentalizing. This can happen with friends as well. Geoffrey Greif has researched men's friendships and categorizes them as:

- Must friends – those friends you may not see often but would drop everything to help one another.

- Trust friends – people you gravitate towards in social situations because they feel comfortable; maybe even friends where everyone lowers their mask (soul friends).

- Just friends – these are "watchin' the game, havin' a Bud" type friends. People who may not know a lot of personal details.

- Rust friends – the guys who go way back (childhood, college, the services). These may fit into one of the other three categories above. Even if they don't, they are forever friends.

Men's friendships may be different from women's because of the way they have been socialized to stifle their feelings and not share. Sports can be one outlet for men. There can be crying, screaming, touching, and all manner of emotions as long as there some kind of ball or weapon involved.

Couple Friends

It can be challenging for couples to find individual friends who are compatible. We are all different in the way we make friends—some make friends with strangers and like to be with a lot of people; others enjoy smaller, more intimate conversations. Shared friendships are amazing if you can find other couples where everyone can be friends. You may even find that you and your spouse bond more after having been with other couples. Getting together in groups of couples, or just with another pair, has the ability to transport us back to childhood. You may eat together, play games, laugh and be silly. It can be a great way to connect to younger parts of your self that need nurturing in that way, especially if you didn't have strong friendships in childhood. And, it may be safer if you are making these friends with your partner as the two of you have a foundation already.

Making friends

Making friends as a child can often be the easiest. You just walk up to some random stranger or someone walks up to you and asks, "Want to be friends?" There you have it—instant buddy. Friends in middle school and even high school are an important part of our development and growth but may be more difficult to make. We all have experienced making friends when we are young. Whether it was easy or difficult for you does not matter in the least when it comes to making friends as an adult. It's simply not the same. When you're grown, friends seem to come from proximity. We go to university together, we met at the yoga studio, or we work in the same office. Perhaps one day you strike up a conversation and then realize you made a friend.

How we make friends depends greatly on our past experience and our confidence in what we offer others. As we heal our past and become more present with our thoughts and emotions, we may find ourselves longing to share who we are becoming with another person. Making friends as an adult you may need to be more proactive in the endeavour—join a group or club, strike up conversations, invite someone for coffee. Someone has to put the invitation out there in order for a friendship to take root, so why not you? Ask questions to get to know the other person, but be mindful of going too far too fast. If this is a friendship for you, it will take time to blossom. If you do have a friend date, be sure to respect the other person by showing up on time and giving lots of notice (if you can) if you have to cancel.

Friendships are built on shared values as much as shared hobbies and interests. Once you make one friend, the group may expand by introducing one another to other friends. Your network of friends begins to grow and then, just when you think your friend-plate is full, you fall in love with a brand-new friend and forget your life before they came into it. Blessed does not begin to describe how I feel having found the friends I have as an adult. They help me explore different parts of myself. They are there for me when I'm struggling just as I am there for them. It's a symbiotic relationship that feeds my soul on a deep level.

We are social creatures. We need one another.

A recent study showing the top indicators of health and longevity are *social interactions* (like talking to someone in the coffee shop) and *having close relationships*. These two beat out quitting smoking, drinking, exercising or losing excess weight when they were absent in people's lives! Who are your friends? The ones you know will be there for you no matter what? The ones who love you in all your weirdness and mess? These are your people. Show up for them, love them, and let them love you back. Forever is a long time. We need to travel with friends.

GOD'S LOVE

A few chapters back, I mentioned that I grew up in a traditional Christian faith. My faith journey has taken me in many directions. Early on, I struggled with the dogma of the church and the ways of thinking that did not make sense to me but were not being discussed from the pulpit. I did go to church off and on as I sought answers to some of life's more difficult questions. But, my experience fell short of my expectations and I had no one guiding my spiritual self so I left to read, study, and explore on my own.

A few years ago, one of our couple friends invited me and my husband to their church. This new church was very different from the experience I had growing up. The service began with worship music that stirred my soul and concluded with a sermon tying the teachings of Jesus to everyday life. I found myself wanting to give this type of church a chance so I returned the next week and then the next. The Pastor spoke each Sunday on issues that seemed so relevant for today—forgiveness, shame, and anxiety; faith, kindness, and patience. The message seemed to always be how to know God in day-to-day life. Love is how we know God. Love is something you do, an action word. You experience love by loving.

Every year this church, that we now attend regularly, embarks on something called Love Week. Imagine for a moment how much love could be spread around the world if everyone did one thing. One act of kindness is done with the sole (or soul) intention of spreading love. God IS love. Whenever I am pulled into moments of skepticism, I look for love in the world. This is what strengthens my belief in God. It is what keeps my faith in humanity. It is why I feel hopeful for the future. Mr. Rogers learned as a boy to look for the helpers in a tragic situation. Whatever you look for, you will find. If you look for helpers, you will find them helping. If you look for love, you will find people loving others. If you look for kindness and compassion, you will find people serving.

When people ask about my faith, I begin with a disclaimer: I was raised Catholic. I think that gives people a perspective of sorts. Namely, I was raised in a specific Christian faith where we had lots of rituals and rites of passages. I listened to the gospel, but I really had no idea what it meant. Catholics get a lot of Mary, the Mother of Jesus, the Pope, and the Vatican. To me, it felt as if there were too many layers between me and God. A lot of rules. In Grade 9, we prepared for Confirmation. It was an opportunity for us to make our own choice about our faith. We were welcomed into the church community (God's family) through our Baptism. As young adults, we got to make our own choice through Confirmation. That meant no church, unless I wanted to go to church.

I didn't.

Until I did.

Going back to church at 18 felt more like a mission. It was after my dad died. I could not seem to make sense of things. I had finished high school and was thinking about my future. I had doubts. I had questions. I began to seek. Along the way, my faith was strengthened as often as it left me. I felt abandoned by God as often as I felt engulfed in God's love. There was a period when I was a self-proclaimed Agnostic. I believed, and still do to some extent, that God is beyond our comprehension. I'm not sure I would ever be comfortable trying to explain God.

What I knew for sure was that I belonged to something bigger than me. A universe that made sense. A universe that was connected and interdependent rather than a series of random accidents. As children, we see everything from our own perspective. It is difficult for children to separate what is real and what is make-believe. God is like any other character—Santa, Easter Bunny, Tooth Fairy. Our understanding of God comes from whatever our parents tell us. This is where most of our faith journeys began. I can remember praying as a child, "I will be good if you grant my wish." God and Fairy Godmother seemed strikingly similar to me as a child.

This message was reinforced in church. Christians are often taught to stack up good deeds to reach God—it never occurred to me that God would reach for me exactly where I was. Things begin to shift for most of us around the age of 7- or 8-years old. Reason brings up a few questions as we begin to understand the world more logically. Unlike the other characters of our childhood, God is still literal; hence, all the questions. We see the church (or our parents) as the authority. Faith can often stick there. We may rely on the church to give us stability. Many people feel comfortable believing things happen for a reason. It is all part of God's plan. So, they stick with what they have been taught. There is solace in familiar faith rituals. Belonging to the church community may be enough. I understand the draw to stick with tradition.

Pushing the Faith Boundaries

There are some who push beyond—some who question. Perhaps we look outside our faith community to other social groups that align more closely with who we are or want to be. Many people at one time or another in their journey may feel they don't belong to the church they attend. Real people seem to understand us more than God. Perhaps we attend out of a sense of obligation, or we are fulfilling an expectation of someone else, maybe our parents or our partner. Or we go to church because that's what we think we're supposed to do. We may even go with no expectation that our spiritual self can or will be met. If we ever question why we attend, doubt around our faith often creeps in. Skepticism is part of the faith journey, but many people may never move beyond this stage. As doubt grows, we may be expected to follow a church doctrine that does not fit with what we believe, so we move outside the box. It can be a tough leg of the journey.

Examining our own beliefs, especially if they do not align with what we've been taught, can push us into disbelief and cynicism. Perhaps our faith journey ends there. We think faith is binary—believers and non-believers. Like everything else in life, it is more nuanced than that. Skepticism is also individualism. Questions such as Who am I? or What is my purpose? are questions of faith. Working through those questions can take the rest of our life. I often hear people say, "I am spiritual, but not religious." I believe what they mean is, "I believe in something bigger, but I don't go to church." Traditional ideas of God may feel too constrictive (or prescriptive) or they may feel excluded.

For those who continue on the journey, there is a yearning for more from their faith. This can happen as a teenager or in mid-life. We begin to look reflectively at the journey of faith itself. "What have I learned?" We begin to realize that the more questions we ask, the more questions there are. Answers to these bigger life questions become a mystery.

- What am I supposed to do?

- What is my purpose, my calling, my vocation?

- Who am I?

- What does my life mean?

- Why am I here?

Asking the question is the key; seeking the answers is a lifelong journey of learning. Life is a paradox—there is joy, and there is suffering. Yet, Genesis tells us that everything God created was good. How can suffering be good? It may take a lifetime, and we still may not be able to answer that question. I've come to accept that some questions are only meant to be asked, not necessarily answered. There is mystery in life and I need to make space for that. Our rational mind prefers the concrete and factual side of life. Limiting our faith to only that part of our mind limits us.

In the story *Les Misérables*, Jean Valjean struggles with these questions of identity. And yet, his dying words bring everything down to this simple truth: "... to love another person is to see the face of God". As I grow older, my faith seems to align more closely with this truth. We are all part of the tapestry, weaving the creation story of love. Perhaps I do not need to figure it out at all. I am loved, and I am love. It matters less what I do and more that I do it with great love. Perhaps, it's as simple (and as complicated) as that.

LIVING SOULFULLY

If I were to say that something was soulful, you would understand what I meant. Food, music, conversations with dear friends—these things can be soulful. They are deep and feel meaningful. You know it when you feel it but it can be difficult to explain. In a world that craves rationality, we tend to look for a definition. We ask, "What is a soul?" However, the soul is not intellectual. It is more than that. It is genuine and intuitive and a lot of other stuff we may feel uncomfortable talking about in our culture today. Soulful is easier to understand because it is an adjective.

In his book *Care of the Soul*, Thomas Moore encourages us to reflect on our life and how it has unfolded. This runs counter to our current-day approaches of trying to figure everything out. The soul is more happenstance. Moore uses the word soul as more of a descriptor rather than a noun, like soulful. I find myself going back to read this book over and over. It is not an easy read, it tackles difficult concepts and ideas about the soul. But it does a good job teaching us how to cultivate a soulful life. And, Moore's writing is closer to that of a poet than a scholar.

Although his credentials are stellar, he writes more from the perspective of imagination than understanding. The soul resides in mystery so Moore leaves room for something to happen to the readers during their engagement with his ideas. Space for finding the meaning in the things that happen in our lives—major changes down to minor, everyday chores. We experience the soul through experiencing life itself. Our culture is beginning to catch up with this idea. The world is so fast and busy, people are experiencing panic and anxiety on a daily basis. We constantly judge ourselves if we are not hustling 24/7. The pressure to succeed is enormous, but succeed at what, exactly? It feels like a race to be successful, live the perfect life, have the perfect body, be the perfect person. Our shadow side is pushed aside and unexamined. Yet, we cannot love ourselves fully without embracing the shadow. The soul does that.

"The human soul is not meant to be understood."

Thomas Moore

"Can you fix me?" is a question I often get when I begin therapy with someone new. Typically, I will joke that I am not a Fairy Godmother. One of the things Moore challenges in his book is this idea of cure vs. care. To cure or fix something means that we never have to deal with it again. Care means bringing attention to it daily. I cannot cure anxiety, and even if I could, it would leave a person pretty vulnerable to that Sabre-Toothed Tiger I mentioned earlier or that Zombie Apocalypse so many movies are made about. For the person experiencing anxiety, it takes regular care to keep it regulated and intervention strategies when it acts up.

Moore also explores the soul by looking at love and belonging, jealousy and envy, narcissism and self-love, power. He asks us to consider, "How many times do we lose an occasion for soul work by leaping ahead to final solutions without pausing to savour the undertones?" In our eagerness to act and move forward, we miss opportunities to know ourselves better through social interactions and soulful conversations with another person, as well as time alone for reflection and deep thinking. These are all ways we can know our selves better as we heal and grow.

The book ends with a section on how to care for the soul. (Spoiler alert: it is by following daily rituals.) The small, daily practices I encouraged you to begin in your last reflective activity. These are things you do with intention towards healing and growth. Disconnecting a little from modern life and reconnecting to the spiritual are just a few ways Moore shows us. It is the essence of our identity, while our ego is our face to the world, our spirit connects the two. Caring for our soul is an important piece. The book holds us individually responsible for caring for the world's soul too. We do that through connection and by being authentic and vulnerable. By living as much from our heart as we do from our head. This is how we move into a state of healing in all aspects of our lives.

Awareness is the soul. Our awareness then becomes our connection to the unlimited energy we experience around us—Chi, Shakti, Spirit. Whatever we call it, it is always there like energy in motion, always expanding. It is what we mean when we say "going with the flow." Triggers that make us aware of our unprocessed trauma are a chance to shift back into healing by focusing less on the thoughts, feelings, and circumstances and more on the self that contains us so that we can witness. Imagine we are a container filled with water, immersed in the ocean. Everything that is part of the ocean can now flow through us. The more space taken up by our unprocessed trauma and emotional wounds, the less space there is to experience all the other things that flow through the ocean.

Imagine a world where we saw everything around us not just as an extension of our self but as literally part of who we are. In Buddhism, the Atman (individual soul) is the same as Brahman (universal soul). How would we treat others or the environment if this were our underlaying premise? How much easier would it be to love our self if we saw that love reflected back to us in every encounter. They seem like big questions when in fact caring for our soul is about simplicity. Mother Theresa would say, "Doing small things with great love" is what makes that thing soulful.

In his book *the untethered soul*, Michael Singer encourages us to relax and release, and deal with what's left in front of us. A meaningful life comes from our willingness to live it. He cautions us about being so externally focused on the bits we cannot control or working endlessly to achieve something; we will miss the life we are capable of experiencing. "Life exists with or without you. It has been going on for billions of years. You simply get the honour of seeing a tiny slice of it."

We live in the here and now, and life does not always fit neatly into the segments we have invented for planning purposes, like days, weeks, and years. That is not to say we should not keep a calendar. We have things we want to do and goals we want to reach, but as long as we are striving forward towards something, we may miss the beauty of the ride. Thriving is about noticing life as we experience it. Hope is knowing we will be okay regardless of our circumstances because we are resilient. We grow and transform as we make meaningful connections in our world.

Living in our purpose means cultivating and using the skills we have been born with. It means serving the people who have shown up on the journey with us. It means living lightly on the planet to leave behind a chance for the next generation. It is not only about our own personal movement up the hierarchy. It is making sure everyone on the planet has the basic needs necessary to transcend and self-actualize and grow. Abraham Maslow says that reaching a state of self-actualization means we must be what we can be. And that our growth needs are ultimately about service to others rather than constantly chasing goals or living in perpetual self-improvement. Being who you are in the world is what it means to live in love.

"Your soul has no agenda. It's not out to make you the best you can be. It's out to fulfill the potential you discover in yourself, which means that you and your soul are in a cooperative venture."

Deepak Chopra

REFLECTIVE ACTIVITY

Finding Harmony

In a previous reflective activity, I invited you to do a visualization to identify the parts of self. Along the way, as you have been reading and answering the questions I asked, you may have discovered parts of yourself that need love and compassion—perhaps your inner child or rebellious teenager. Perhaps you've met a part of you that was hurt or disappointed and is now an unintentional barrier to healing. Connecting to one of those parts can be done through an exercise of Free Writing.

The idea is to get into a stream of consciousness that is beyond your prefrontal cortex or rational mind so you can experience these parts from a new and different perspective. For this activity, set aside 3-5 minutes. Go to a place where you will not be interrupted; a place that invokes a sense of calm. Begin writing and do not stop. Do not lift your pen, reread or cross things out. Just keep going and see what comes up—an image, a memory; specific thoughts or emotions. Something that will give you some insight into what needs your healing attention.

Begin by writing, **"The part of me that needs some healing attention is..."**

If you met a part of yourself and want to take an interaction further, write back and forth to that part of yourself. You may use different colour pens: one for you today, one for the other part of yourself—past or future—that you may have met. If the part is a child, you can write their part with your non-dominant hand, perhaps using a writing device a child would use like a crayon.

You may also want to use Empty Chair rather than writing back and forth. Do the Free Writing first, then set up two seats that face each other. In the chair, you picture the part of yourself you want to speak to and connect with. Imagine them in the empty chair. An old picture of yourself at that age can help. If it's a feeling you want to connect with, give it a form.

Decide who will speak first. If it's today you, explain your feelings, thoughts, and understanding of the situation and that you are there with love and compassion. After you've shared your side of things, you move to the other chair and respond to what you just said, from that person's perspective, taking on their role. You may move back and forth between the chairs several times to continue the dialogue. If it's a younger part that has big feelings (perhaps they are angry and want to yell or blame), check in with today you and how you feel about their words and emotions.

The idea of this activity is to ensure you know the parts of yourself that may be resistant to going with you into the next section of the book, which is focused on transformation and growth. Every part needs to feel safe for that journey.

CHAPTER SEVEN

CHANGING THE *Story*

How to use the voice you found to live the life you want

"In the end, we'll all become stories."

Margaret Atwood

Have you ever poured something fizzy into a glass and have the contents overflow? I think we all have. What if that idea of overflow applies to us too? I use clinical counselling hypnotherapy periodically in my practice to help people reach down into their subconscious minds. Only so much can be learned about ourselves using our rational brains. Our conscious mind is only the tip of the iceberg. We all have much more under the surface—emotions, creativity, pain, bias, old stories and patterns, and the parts of self that are stuck in them. Much of what makes us *us* resides in our subconscious.

Regardless of why we use hypnosis, I typically begin by bringing the person into a deep state of relaxation. I do this by having them breathe deeply into various parts of their body, beginning with their feet and going all the way up to their head. Like in the activity you did in Chapter 5, I ask people to use their breath as a way of locating stress, tension, trauma, or pain. I ask them to inhale into a specific part of the body, loosen anything that has been built up there, and then release it on the exhale. The idea is to make space for relaxation—feelings of calm, tranquility, and serenity. Just like you cannot pour from an empty cup, you cannot pour *into* a full cup either.

As we continue through our life on a journey of healing and growth, it is important to check in with our self on where our capacity is. Contemplate, on a regular basis, what is taking up space in your life that you don't need, and then let it go to make space for the things you *do* need. Your calendar can be a place where it is obvious what things are taking up space in your life. If there is too much of doing for others and not enough rest and recovery, your cup will overflow. Likewise, if you are spending too much time in your own world and not enough time in service to others, you will not be filling yourself up with the energy that is generated by interacting with other people.

As we continue to craft our life story, we need to figure out what to let go of or put down. We also need to figure out what fills us up. Our purpose is an extension of us. It grows from our character. It is more than just our day-to-day job. Whether this daily work is formal or informal, we know we have to show up each day and do it. The question is how do we do it? Is it from a place of joy?

When you squeeze an orange, you'll get orange juice. We expect that what is inside the orange will come out when we apply pressure. What comes out when I am squeezed? When the stress and hurriedness of everyday life squeezes me, how do I react? When you are stressed, do you react with anger and frustration? Or, can you find perspective in the moment and react in a way the situation requires? Can you give to others when they are hurting? Can you fill them up with kindness and encouragement? Most importantly, can you give that love and compassion to yourself?

Our life story is an extension of our character. Who we are and what is important to us in the world is the foundation for our purpose. We all have stuff from our past that seems to carry with us. It is important to look at those experiences from time to time to see how they have served us. We all have stuff we have to work through. Some challenges leave behind a residue of guilt or shame. We don't always handle everything as well as we would like. We are human, so we second guess and judge ourselves. It is only through examination and contemplation that we can decide to make space for the things we value most in the world.

THE BLACK DOG(S)

You may have heard the story of the black dog. The metaphor is that this black dog represents depression. It's believed to have originated with Winston Churchill, but it goes back much further than that. Shakespeare talks about it in his work. Even as far back as Ancient Rome, the poet Horace talked about his "dark companion."

If depression can be described as a black dog, anxiety would be a guard dog. I think of the black dog of depression like a Newfoundland dog—big, slow, needy. It makes you tired because you have to drag it everywhere. The guard dog of anxiety is more like a wolf. It is on hyper-alert. It may have woken up during a time in your life when you were unsafe in an effort to protect you. But now, it may be pacing and jittery, barking endlessly because it perceives everything as a threat. These dogs seem to be showing up in our society and our lives more and more. We may feel unsafe (anxious) and hopeless (depressed). I believe hope can be found in knowing we are not alone.

Most of us know the story of Dr. Jekyll and Mr. Hyde. We tend to think about these characters as separate, even though we know they are the same person. Dr. Jekyll makes a potion in the story, which I always assumed was meant to kill Mr. Hyde. Not so. Dr. Jekyll makes the potion so he can express the shadow side of himself. Think about the name he gives to this other character—Hyde. Dr. Jekyll is the primary person. That is why he talks in the first person. "I looked in the mirror and saw Hyde, the pleasures I sought in my disguise."

Mr. Hyde does not care about the things Dr. Jekyll cares about as a man of stature—wealth, success, friendship. Jekyll needs an outlet so he creates Hyde in his laboratory. This is an extreme example, but many people I know struggling with anxiety and depression are ashamed of their feelings. There is still immense stigma related to mental health issues. We try to push it down. We put our "together self" out there in a form similar to Dr. Jekyll—respectable, professional—while we hide the shadow. Doing that gives the shadow a tremendous amount of power over us.

I love analogies. They can be very helpful in trying to make sense of the world. If we think about depression as a black dog or anxiety as a guard dog, it is easier to figure out how to work with them. Rather than thinking about getting rid of (or hiding) these parts of our self, we need to learn how to live with them in harmony. This starts by seeing them, understanding them, and ultimately accepting that this part is part of us. Like training a puppy or a rescue, think about how this would apply if we were to shift our perspective on anxiety and depression. You start training by getting to know one another. The more you know your anxiety or depression, the easier it will be to hold space for the experiences and allow them to pass through you. You can negotiate with your anxiety or depression if you have a relationship with them. What are their characteristics? What are times of the day when they may be more difficult to handle? Get to know them more intimately. Once you know, you can set up rules for interacting with them.

If you think about taking care of your depression like you would take care of a pet, it can be easier to prioritize self-care. You would take your pet for a walk, even on days when you don't feel like it, because you know it's good for them. Adding moments of self-care into your schedule is a way of caring for those parts of self. We're told that exercise is beneficial for people navigating depression, but it's often the last thing you want to do when you feel low. Commit to caring for your depression like you would a beloved pet—getting out of bed to take them out for a walk, even if it feels like a slog,

You may not feel you're getting anything out of it but you do it because self-care is *not* a luxury. You can be proud of yourself when you have successfully managed your anxiety or depression in everyday situations. Did you go to that get-together even though depression did not want to go? Give yourself a high five. Did you ask a difficult question or stick up for yourself in a situation where your anxiety was freaking out? You deserve recognition. It is not an easy thing to do, go you! Positive reinforcement goes a long way. These tips for managing anxiety and depression may sound simplistic, but they are hard to implement. Patience and consistency are key.

TELLING YOUR STORY

There is power in telling your story out loud. You are using both your rational and emotional mind to tell a story. Formulating it in words brings it to life. As the words flow out of you, the story loosens its grip somehow. There is power in having a witness as well. Especially if you felt alone in parts of your story. The other person does not need to say anything; they just need to be present. Even if that other person is another part of you or your core self. Consider some of the things that prevent you from telling your story:

- What if you cannot speak your story?

- What if there are no words for the trauma you experienced?

- What if the story is generational? A wound you inherited that is not yours alone.

- What if you were too young to have the necessary language? The trauma can keep you stuck at the age you were when you experienced it.

There are times when using language is limiting. The limitations become apparent when people are going through the motions in talk therapy but cannot find the healing they seek. The wounds of trauma can change who we are, attacking us at our core—how we see ourselves and our relation to the world. Because we are injured, we consult experts for help. Medical experts use medication to manage symptoms. Psychologists use cognitive-behavioural therapy to help manage thoughts and feelings. Therapists help you find your voice and tell your story. The combination of these things can be helpful for many but limiting for others.

Humans are a complex system, similar to a computer. The first line of defence for the IT Helpdesk is to ask: "Did you try turning it off and on?" That can be enough. There were too many programs open. The system got overloaded. Programs need to be upgraded to continue working effectively. Occasionally the system just needs to be unplugged. When things go haywire and the IT specialist has little idea how to fix the problem, they reboot the entire system. Rebooting means scaling everything back to the basics and reinstalling the programs. Traditional practitioners and therapies are the first lines of defence that help us manage presenting problems. In the case of a soul injury or a trauma wound, we may require a reboot.

The reason you feel lost or trapped in your story is because there are parts of you still living in the trauma. Parts of you that are stuck in that time. They do not need you to tell their story because they are still living it. They need you to rescue them because no amount of talk therapy or medication or goal setting is going to heal them. Healing at a soul level requires *more* than talking. We do not want to limit healing with language or filter it through the lens of judgement. We do need the mind, but more as a guide in the process. The conscious mind can open the door to the subconscious mind. We can travel through time and rescue the parts of our self that are stuck there.

In the movie *The Iron Giant*, there is a scene at the end (spoiler alert) when the Iron Giant is blown apart. The audience thinks he is dead. But then you see the various parts, strewn across the world, begin rolling back toward one another. The audience feels hopeful the Iron Giant will be whole again as the parts come together. That is what healing our soul looks like.

Beth's Story

Having experienced childhood sexual abuse, Beth felt broken. She entered therapy because she met someone and desperately wanted to be in a "normal" relationship, which she had never experienced because she was too ashamed. Logically she knew she was not to blame, but the wound was deep. She could tell her story but felt something was anchoring her to that time and place. Trauma healing is difficult and important work, but it is painful. Many people dread the idea of working through it. Beth could not imagine spending time in the past. The intention is not to go back to relive the story but rather to end the trauma story. It is going back only to rescue the part of yourself that is still there—bringing the parts safely into the present and integrating them into your whole self.

We used hypnotherapy and guided visualization to connect to her inner strength and wisdom—the wise guide who had brought her through as best she could. Then, we helped Beth find a safe (calm and serene) space that would anchor her in the present so she would not feel over-whelmed when she met her younger self. Finally, we ventured back to find her lost little girl by pulling on an old memory of a time when she felt safe but alone. She imagined herself at 5 years old, in her nightgown, playing with her dolls before bed. As an adult, she knows that little girl has been experiencing things no child should.

In the visualization, I asked her to make eye contact with the girl and smile. She imagined the little girl smiling back with trust. She told her she was safe now. Her adult part would take care of the child part. Beth knew the little girl was not to blame. The idea seemed ridiculous. She could see that her fear of dating was an old fear of being hurt when she was vulner-able. The rest of our time together in therapy was practicing doing things in the present that felt vulnerable and getting to the other side. The more she untangled feeling vulnerable from being hurt, the easier it was to take risks until she felt ready to extend the practice to dating.

If you venture down the path of trauma healing, be sure to find a trauma-informed practitioner. Take several sessions (as many as you need) to build trust so it does not feel overwhelming. It is always healing to go at your own pace with a lot of compassion and self-care along the way. As you feel yourself healing, you begin to tell a new story—the one of triumph over adversity.

I recently sat with an older woman whose 102-year old mother was in the hospital healing from many broken bones, including a broken neck. Our conversation about her mother's health turned to a broader discus-sion about death as a part of life. She said to me, "Everything comes to earth to die." Then, she looked around the room and pointed out some examples—this wood, this table, this fabric. She appreciated the spirit of the object that had come to die and took more pleasure in the things around her with that philosophy. That was a profound concept for me. I thought, perhaps that is the purpose of our lives too.

When I would look at my young son, see his beautiful face, his teasing smile, his innocence, I would grieve a little—how I will miss this little boy when he is grown. His childhood and youth are simply the beginning chap-ters in the story of the man he will become. You cannot truly appreciate what is around you unless you have contemplated losing it. In this under-standing of grief, we can find the skill to truly live in praise of life. Knowing things will die is what allows me to fully love this moment, because I know how precious and fleeting it is. We must love the end of something to love it fully. It shows the end (death) as part of the process—one more change in our ever-changing lives.

It's been said that our story *begins* after the trauma. If that is the case, then the new story can be one of healing and hope. Tragedy can give us a unique perspective. We are broken but often broken open to new possibilities. Healing comes in putting things back together, but it is also a chance to not put *all* the pieces back. Some stories are not worth retelling. The new story of hope and healing is an opportunity to identify the hero, the battle, and the victory. We can write and rewrite the story as we go. We can live our lives as a story of inspiration. In an ego world, we only think of ourselves. If we put our story out there for praise, sympathy, or likes and clicks, then the value of our story is only experienced externally. It stands alone as a thing that happened to us and does not allow space for anything deeper. The soul's story is selfless because the soul understands that we are all connected. My story connects to your story. Seeing our stories as connected highlights the obligation we have to one another through generations.

Death is a change, but then, everything in life changes. Our choice is in how we choose to see it. Without getting too philosophical, the present moment is all we ever have. We can only experience the past through memory, and the future does not really exist. By this, I mean there will always be a future moment. The future eludes us, so we cannot live there. We can plan (hope for the future) and reflect (learn from the past) in an effort to bring all possibilities together in the present moment and fall a little more deeply into who we are.

In 1963, Betty Friedan published a book called *The Feminine Mystique*. She had interviewed women throughout the late 1950s who were unhappy with their lives but could not really say why they were unhappy. Friedan called it "the problem with no name." In this century, I have encountered many men and women experiencing the same thing. Like the suburban housewives of the 1950s, people look at their life and think, "I should be happy". Especially if they have achieved the life society lays out for us—a good job, a home, married with kids. If we are globally conscious, we can look at our lives and our opportunities and wonder what in the world we have to be unhappy about. This leads to self-judgement and a pick-your-self-up-by-the-bootstraps attitude. "Just think positive," we read. And the problem with no name continues.

Once it had a voice, however, the women Friedan interviewed were honest about the fact that they craved for something more. They loved their lifestyle (material comfort), loved their husband and children. Yet, they yearned for something that could fulfill them as individuals. Much of their lives fulfilled their basic physiological and safety needs. However, they often felt as if they did not belong to anything bigger than the day-to-day experiences they had. Although they did not know what it was, there was no place for growth in their daily lives. We all need to strive for self-actualization in order to feel content.

TRANSITIONING THE STORY

We already explored how the KonMari Technique for organizing your space and getting rid of things works when you ask whether or not that thing sparks joy. In Chapter 2, you saw me use this question with my client Charlie, who lost his wife and wanted to keep up his space. In an episode where the item did not necessarily spark joy but had sentimental value, Kondo asked, "Do you want to bring this with you in the future?" Such a great question for so many things in life we carry, including old parts of our story. Perhaps an even better question to be asking when it comes to our sentimental attachment to the parts of our story that no longer serve us.

The story of your life is waiting to be completed, so this question is as much about big healing moments as it is about day-to-day maintenance. It is not only about our physical stuff. What old stories or characters, or character traits, do you want to bring with you into your future? This is a transition. And, like the analogy of This Old House, transition happens more slowly and focuses on the internal stuff. Like any project, we do the work in stages. Working through each one requires reflection; and, sometimes, decision-making. First, we must go through the ending of something. We must give this part space. Even if you are excited about the next phase in your life, there is still loss.

Letting go of the things that we no longer need for our journey is an important part of the process in changing the story. Each time we decide to do something new, put something down, move forward in a different direction, we are in the process of transformational learning—our way of being in the world changes. The lens we look through, especially if it is a lens of healing and love, shifts our perspective so much that the way we now interpret the world is different. This lens is our wise mind and becomes the compass for navigating our future actions. Every time we allow an emotion to have a voice—to allow and process— every reframing or modified attitude or world view produces a different result in our lives. They forge new pathways in the brain so that our brain is literally changing.

Our brains are pliable. Neuro-linguistic programming is the connection between thoughts, language, and behaviour. It teaches us that once this transformational learning has happened, it not only changes our behaviour, but the way we process information completely changes. Now, rather than meeting resistance or feeling as if you should be doing something to move forward, you simply move through it. Getting used to this new way of being in the world is what I describe as getting your sea legs. It is a place to slow down and catch your breath. Anxiety may be high as you grapple with issues of identity. *Who am I now?* That brings the final stage, which is a new beginning. A new chapter, or if you like, a complete rewrite of the chapters that preceded this one of *now*.

Thinking of transition as a stage may indicate moving through the process rather than leaning into the process. It's different. It is not checking the boxes on a list but instead asking difficult questions or making difficult decisions about what to do next. The journey means looking backward to see how far you've come. It also means setting your sights on what the future will be, what you want, and who you are. This is a place where you may say thank you for everything you are moving on from. Everything teaches us something. Those lessons can be gentle, or they can be tough. How you have changed and grown through each of those things has brought you here.

Inevitably, you will want to keep some of who you have become. Some things you may want to let go of. Either way, gratitude is like a reconciliation. It helps us get to a place where we are not attached to the events in our past. We see our experiences for what they are and what they have given us. And then, we move forward. For me, there is a neutral zone that has become about generating energy. I need the energy to move my life forward and forge new territory. Mid-life can often bring a reawakening, as can any transitional time in your life. There is an opportunity to reinvent yourself and your life. Yes, it is scary, but I would argue it is worth it. You are a different person now, with all you have experienced. Some people say life is a lesson, but I think it is a test. We have to be put to the test to learn the lesson. In order to change, we must reflect and evaluate as we go.

WRITING THE NEXT CHAPTER

When I opened my practice as a therapist, I worried I would not have the motivation of work deadlines to get things done. What would keep me at my desk? After working for someone else for decades, would I have the self-discipline? Although I had some flexibility in my jobs before, there were still expectations that I would show up most days somewhere between 9-5. There were committees and projects. All had hard deadlines. Except for scheduled client meetings, those are gone. Where do we get our motivation and validation in life?

We all have goals we would like to achieve. Like everyone else, I am proud of myself when I succeed and disappointed when I don't. Even though I see myself as independent, the truth is I'm human and miss the positive reinforcement I used to get at work. It feels good to have someone recognize us when we've accomplished a task or stuck something out when things were difficult. We have all done things we are proud of, whether it's finishing a project, losing weight, running a marathon, or raising great kids. It feels nice when someone else is proud of us too. Validation from another person is a way to feel seen and heard. It helps us feel valuable. That what we are doing is important. **We matter.**

Looking back gives you more perspective. You can see the accomplishment amid all the other things going on in your life—competing deadlines or priorities, sick kids, cold weather. All the times you could have bailed on the gym but you showed up anyway. Being proud of yourself in the moment is different than looking back fondly on accomplishments. You may feel proud that you showed up every day this week to the gym. Being validated helps us feel as if we belong, and it boosts our self-esteem. That is why telling your goals to someone else can help you stay the course. You are now accountable for what you said you would do. Validation from others is nice, but witnessing and validating for ourselves builds our intrinsic motivation. We begin to do things for the sake of completing them rather than for the reward of praise. We are doing the things we set out to do, and we can feel good about that.

Think about it from the point of view of regret. Bronnie Ware was a palliative care nurse who wrote *The Top Five Regrets of Dying*. No one wants to have regrets on their deathbed. Yet, how often do we think about what our future self will say about the life we are living? Will *Future You* be impressed with the life you are living today? Being a grief and trauma therapist, I see people struggle every day with regret. We all know we will not get it right all the time. Hell, probably most of the time. None of us wants to regret that we did not at least try. If I hung out my shingle for private practice and was unsuccessful, I could live with that, especially if I worked daily to make it viable. At least I took a chance. I never want *Future Me* to look back and think, "What if?"

Of course, we all have regrets. We all make mistakes. I find myself wanting to impress *Future Me* by showing up in my life day after day and giving it everything I've got. I want *Future Me* to look back and say, "Damn. You lived well. Thank you, *Past Me!*" Looking back, what do you want your future self to say about your life? Often, we look back and wonder how we have gotten to this point in our life? It seems that many times we are where we are in life not because we have methodically planned things out but because we have taken opportunities as they have come up.

Our journey to this point may be one of happenstance, which is not necessarily a bad thing. However, for some people (often around 40), we are high enough on the life ladder to see the landscape clearly, and we may be surprised by what we see. The risk of getting down and climbing a different ladder at that point may be daunting. It is why we get stuck. Our heart is telling us one thing *you don't belong here, get down!* while our head is telling us another *you have bills to pay and mouths to feed, stay put!* It's a disorienting dilemma. How do we begin to reconcile that contra-diction? Surveying the landscape is a place to start. It includes reflecting on all areas of our life—health (physical, mental, emotional, intellectual, financial); relationships (spouse, kids, parents, friends, colleagues, and the environment); vocation (paid work, volunteer, hobbies).

Defining success in these areas invites ongoing reflection—How am I doing? Am I at my best? Am I making time for my life priorities? One way to tell is to keep a time journal. It is similar to a food journal, but it records time dedicated each day to various priorities. The first thing to do is get a sense of where your time is going and then reorganize the day to ensure your time is equal to your priorities. Most of us spend so much of our time making a living; we don't have the time (or energy) to make a life. No one wishes they made more money or spent more time at the office when they are dying. They wish they had risked more, loved more, spent more time making a difference in the world.

At a time when the world feels unpredictable, taking control of our life can be empowering. It can feel hopeful to know we are striving to be our best self and living our lives to our fullest potential. Perspective can stimulate options. I believe once you put something out there, no matter how crazy it seems, the universe will conspire to help you achieve it. We are co-creators. We need to spend less time worrying about the how and spend more time bringing what we want into our conscious mind and saying, "Yes!"

SELF-AUTHORSHIP

Self-authorship is the ability to make meaningful connections between our self and our experiences. It is realizing that we are more than just our thoughts, feelings, or even our experiences. How we make meaning in our lives depends on our ability to see ourselves as the authors of our own stories. From Robert Kegan's work on levels of consciousness to Marcia Baxter Magolda's refining of this concept, self-authorship can be defined simply as "the internal capacity to define one's beliefs, identity and social relations." Of course, this assumes that people go through a process of reflection to determine the lens through which they will see the world, independent of the messages they may have gotten from their families or society.

Kegan's levels of mind include the developmental parts of our childhood—seeing ourselves as separate from our caregivers, then moving towards reason and abstract thinking. He saw self-authoring as a way the mind handles multiple roles and expectations and takes responsibility for our own lives. This is where I see people struggling. The meaning schemes they have grown up with may not fit anymore. They want to break free from values and ideologies that belong to their family of origin so they can create their own. It can be challenging to do, however. Fear of rejection may trigger an insecure attachment response. The status quo seems the easier way.

A trauma response that says you need to be small (or invisible) to blend in can be difficult to break free of. But, if a person can push through that and consider their own values, then a self-transforming mind is possible. It happens infrequently because there is so much pressure to stay the same. People who have a deep desire for change need to be able to step outside their own story. They need to understand the interconnections between different people and be able to see themselves and others within the systems we have created as interdependent. That is when transformation is possible. That is when a new story for how we can live in the world begins to take shape.

This can be especially difficult for people currently experiencing trauma. Whether it is bullying at work or violence in your relationship, you can transform your situation by doing things differently than you have before. Of course, you cannot do it alone. Reaching out for support and help to escape traumatic circumstances is key. Find someone you trust, even if it is a social agency providing support for people in your situation. If you recognize your situation as a generational response, just for a moment, imagine you can do something different. Just imagining a possibility, even if you don't know exactly how you will get there, makes it possible to transform the situation and escape into a new story.

Transformation happens in three ways—our belief system (cognitive), our identity (intrapersonal) and our relationships with others (interpersonal). Making decisions means considering all three. It also means trusting your own internal voice, building a foundation of values and a philosophy by which to live your life and learning to live authentically according to those convictions. What you believe becomes how you live your life. You have become the author of your life story, which can then influence the story of this generation.

- **Are you living with courage?** The number one regret of dying people is that they wished they had been true to themselves rather than living for the expectations of other people or society.

- **Are you working to the exclusion of other things?** The second regret was that people wished they had not worked so hard. There are so many other things in life that need our attention.

- **Are you in touch with friends and significant people in your life?** Friends and family need as much attention from us as our daily tasks of living and making a living. Dying people wish they had spent more time with the people they love.

- **Are you expressing how you feel?** Can you be authentic and vulnerable? Those who were dying wished they had the courage to be more authentic with their feelings. *I love you. I'm sorry. Can you forgive me? That hurt my feelings.* These are hard to say, but they bring us closer to one another.

GENERATIONAL TRAUMA

Although this book is for you and your healing journey, I would be remiss if I did not talk about generational trauma. Generational trauma is different from the acute trauma someone experiences from a single traumatic event like a car accident. Trauma can be chronic or ongoing—child or domestic abuse, or prolonged exposure to other types of violence, including bullying. This type of trauma usually morphs into complex trauma when a person is exposed to multiple events, causing multiple trauma wounds. The person experiencing the trauma does not have time, or perhaps the ability, to integrate and make sense of what is happening. In cases where the person feels threatened, their anxiety (fight/flight/freeze response) may be constantly engaged, which places a great deal of stress on the system. An overloaded system of stress can mean normal everyday interactions are compromised. In other words, it is difficult to live your life—everything gets filtered through the lens of trauma and can invoke a traumatic response.

Think about how a mother may respond to her children if her system is in a constant state of threat. Imagine the child feels that tension in their nervous system and is told, "Everything is okay, don't worry." That will cause the child to grow up mistrusting their own nervous system response. No validation of emotional trauma in the nervous system means unresolved trauma and trauma wounds will travel with them into adulthood. This is a form of indirect trauma. It is understandable in that circumstance to imagine the child may grow up with trauma wounds. But is it only the environment that causes trauma? Not necessarily. Brain Sciences published a research article in 2018 that looked at the effects of trauma on DNA and found that trauma can pass down from generation to generation. Trauma is both nature and nurture.

We may all have generational trauma to some degree. These can be in your own personal family stories or whispers of stories—addiction, abandonment, adoption, stories of shame. They can also be stories of trauma on a global scale—holocausts and genocide, residential schools, slavery, pandemics. A study called *Wounds of History* shows links between generational trauma and our attachment style. It makes sense that children experience insecure attachment patterns if their caregivers carry trauma wounds. In fact, the study showed that trauma is passed on through four basic psychological pathways: the parent may experience vicarious trauma at certain stages of their child's development. Specifically, at ages they were when they experienced trauma.

Imagine a 5-year-old child having an emotional meltdown over something his dad deems "ridiculous". If dad experienced abuse at that age, he might find it difficult to regulate his own emotions in the situation. Instead, it may trigger him back to his own unresolved trauma experience and result in him lashing out at the child. In addition, children of traumatized adults may find themselves assuming responsibility for their parents. In essence, the child becomes the caregiver. In the case above, it may be that the child learns to calm Dad rather than the other way around.

Alternatively, parenting patterns may repeat—Dad treats his kid the way he was treated for the same behaviour. This is where we may see patterns of abuse and an it-worked-for-me attitude. Finally, communication around issues of trauma continues. If Dad comes from a family where boys cannot express feelings, he may continue that by his own reaction to emotional outbursts. Whether it is because the adult is preoccupied and less able to create secure parent-child relationships or has unresolved trauma resulting in triggers, these pathways are direct and indirect ways parents unintentionally keep the story of trauma going.

Transformation is possible, however. When I was studying adult education, I was intrigued by the work of Jack Mezirow on transformational learning. Rather than simply a function of thinking or remembering, Mezirow says learning not only changes how we think but who we are. That said, remembering is important to the transformational process because "if an interpretation is not remembered, it implies thinking but not learning. Interpretation here means offering a meaning of something. Interpretation can also mean drawing inferences from or explaining something." The point is not to forget the story. Rather, through the retelling and reframing of the story, we can understand and transform it. We can draw new meaning from it. It is not something that continues to wound us. And, how we heal our own personal trauma wounds is how we heal generational trauma.

Vern Neufeld Redekop's work with communities of people who had experienced the Rwandan genocide was called the Justice of Blessing model. It was meant to show that survivors who focused on cognitive reframing—the ability to look at their stories through a new lens of meaning—were able to heal their communities. Healing also included spiritual disciplines and practices that stretched beyond coping strategies. Survivors were being empowered to re-establish their communities in ways that fostered security and personal agency. The trauma experienced on an individual level would also be healed on a communal level—strength in numbers with everyone telling a new story. The story was one of hope for the future and future generations.

Keri Lawson-Te Aho also published her work on using re-narration of trauma stories as the starting point for healing. Her work was with Māori women from a community in Aotearoa, New Zealand and found that the telling of their stories reframed as opportunities for self-determination and ongoing healing meant these were now stories of resilience.

It can often take a generation for people in these communities to fully embrace the new narrative. It does not dismiss the trauma. Rather, it gives it a voice. That voice needs to be witnessed and validated to be healed.

It is not easy, but it is possible for healing to happen on a big scale. It begins with us. Each one of us is responsible for healing our own trauma wounds. That has massive implications on a global scale. Like all forms of trauma, generational trauma can be healed through safe attachments and nervous system regulation. More importantly, it is about rewriting the story through the lens of meaning-making.

Many narratives pass through our culture. In essence, working through the trauma, you become a transitional character—changing the narrative to one of healing that can then be passed down to future generations. Yes, it means you have a heavier burden, but who changes the story if not us? The way we interpret and tell our stories is our hope for the future. It is up to us to change the narrative for future generations.

REFLECTIVE ACTIVITY

Life Dimensions

Take a look at the various areas of your life (see chart below) and ask yourself—what would it look like if this area of life was a 10/10? What emotional cues inside me would tell me I was still living at a 10 in this area—how would I feel, who would be sharing it with me, what would I be doing in this area each day, week, month, year?

Once you have defined what that looks like, rate yourself where you feel you are now. Go back through the areas and determine where you are on a scale from 1-10. Ask yourself (regardless of the number) —why so high? Even if it is only a 3 right now, you want to build on things you are already doing. Why a 3 and not a 1?

Where are your quick wins? For example, having a savings account may be a financial goal, so open an account and put in $10—BAM, now you have savings! How can you move up quickly in some of these areas? There will be some areas that need more of your attention than others. Decide where you want to focus to see if you can move up the satisfaction scale in some of these categories.

Physical
Nutrition, Movement, Sleep, Medical, Basic Physiological Needs (food, shelter, warmth)

Psychological
Therapy, Support, Journaling, Reading, Connection, Nature (gardening, walking)

Professional
Learning Opportunities, Mentorship, Boundaries, Support from Colleagues

Emotional
Trauma Healing (forgives, amends), Regulation (holding space, breathwork)

Personal
Friendship, Finances, Goals & Dreams, Self-Care Routine, Time to Yourself

Spiritual
Time for Reflection, Prayer, Volunteering & Service, Connecting to a Higher Power

CHAPTER EIGHT

LIVING WITH *Purpose*

How to use hope as the fuel for your future

"The meaning of life is to find your gift.
The purpose of life is to give it away."

Pablo Picasso

Go back to the image of interconnectedness and see it as a bucket sub-merged in the ocean. The whole ocean flows through me—I am part of the whole. Often, we live as if our bucket, the possibility for our life, is suspended *over* the ocean. We may be close enough to know possibility for our life is there; we may even want to emerge ourselves. Stuck is when we feel contained in our lives, connected only to what can fit in our bucket. We can feel limited. If we think of a concept like abundance, I may ladle and hoard what I can fit into my bucket above the ocean—working hard to gather what I need. Then imagine I submerge my bucket into the ocean so everything can flow through me. That is what it means to live in a world that is in constant motion.

The idea that we are connected to everything we dream of having in life requires a few changes on our part. First, we have to learn to trust. We have to believe that the universe is abundant and that everything flows. As long as we stay emerged in the ocean of possibility, we are connected. We trust that everything will flow to and then through each of us. Next, we need to truly understand our purpose. This is not only so that we achieve what we want on an individual level. We need to figure out how each of us can make use of the gifts and talents we have and how to structure our lives to be of service to others. As I was trying to connect to my purpose, I realized that my purpose was trying to connect to me. Every time I was drawn to people or certain opportunities, it felt like I had come home.

Lastly, and probably the most difficult of all, we have to believe we are worthy. We need to build, hone, and share our skills with those around us, as if we have something valuable inside us that we just have to share. We need to believe that there is value in the lessons of our life experiences so that we can go through the process of transformational healing.

Just a year out of high school, I was inspired to teach. I went to college with a focus on elementary-level teaching. Although I knew early into the program that a classroom teaching career didn't quite fit, I knew education was the right path. I set my intention on figuring out where exactly I did fit. I searched for my purpose through formal and informal learning—university, workshops, self-directed reading. As I began to connect with new ideas and new ways of knowing, I instinctively wanted to share what I learned with others. That deep yearning to share what I had learned was my purpose trying to connect with me. Ultimately, that is what teaching is: inspiring others to be curious and connecting them to new ideas. It is helping others explore meaning in their own lives and looking at things through a new lens or with a different perspective. It is challenging what we have been taught, to make sure we are exercising our critical thinking muscles regularly.

Most importantly, it is about being in love with the process. I set the intention to live my life from a place of purpose and still be able to pay my bills ("real world" constraints). Those things do not have to conflict. My intention to live my purpose and still manage my financial obligations helps me think outside the box about what is possible. Living in a world of possibility is emerging fully into the ocean and allowing purpose to flow. Right now is the right time to contemplate and set intentions. Once you get clear on what it is you want in your life, emerge your bucket in the ocean and allow the flowing to begin.

Who we are goes beyond what is happening in our minds. It goes deeper than the voices in our heads. It also goes beyond how we feel. For example, I can be happy, and I can be sad; neither says anything about who I am. It is simply how I am feeling (internal) in any given situation (external). I am more than just my feelings, just as I am more than my thoughts or my physical body. There are three interdependent realms necessary for helping us discover and connect to our authentic self: the physical (body), intellectual (mind) and spiritual (soul). The real me exists somewhere in the middle. Remember the Venn diagram from Chapter 2? I exist at the point where all three intersect—mind, body, spirit. Reaching inward to connect with our authentic self includes connecting to the world through all three realms.

If we can appreciate ourselves from all three perspectives—mind, body, spirit—it may help quiet the voices that dominate our minds to give the other two a chance. Our authentic self does not identify with one thought or feeling in particular. It goes beyond the voices in our head or what we are feeling in any particular moment. It is deeper than our day-to-day experiences. Much attention these days is paid only to the mind and what we think. It is a very important part of the process, no doubt. But there is more.

When I was studying counselling, I connected deeply with narrative therapy. The underlying theory is that people are experts in their own lives. Our lives are our stories and we are the author. Dr. Martin Luther King Jr.'s *I have a dream* speech is arguably one of the most familiar of our generation. According to historians, it was not even the speech King prepared to deliver that day. The people who stayed to hear him speak knew that, in the end, all that mattered was keeping the dream alive. They needed to hear that again—the reassurance to keep going, to persevere. Dr. King began to describe what his dream would look like once it was realized. His conviction both fueled and ended his life. People may look at accomplishing a dream as success. We set a goal or intention and achieve it successfully but I believe there is a difference between success and significance.

Although Dr. King did not achieve the success of his dream in his lifetime, his life was one of significance. He was part of a bigger story—a thread in the dream's tapestry. Like Moses, he did not live to see the promised land. His purpose was in standing for something bigger than himself. He stood for justice saying, "Injustice anywhere is a threat to justice everywhere." That sentiment is still working itself out in western culture. Maybe we will see it in our lifetime, maybe not. Our role is to pick up the torch and carry it through our leg of the journey.

Our dreams shape who we are and who we become. It is in the becoming that we have the opportunity to live a life of significance. My dream is to be a healer, yours may be doctor, social worker, teacher. Our individual success comes in being significant to those around us. My dream involves being of service yet that cannot be achieved without a significant positive influence on those I serve. When we define our life based on who we want to become and what kind of influence we want to have on the world, the dream becomes bigger than just us as individual.

Success is not so much a destination but a journey. I heard professor Matthew L. Saunders speak once on his book *Becoming a Learner*. He talked about obtaining a degree in this way—if you go to school for a degree, you may or may not be educated; but if you go to school to be educated, you will get a degree. He saw the degree as a by-product of the education. The degree is not the thing to be achieved in and of itself; rather, it is the journey to the degree he sees as key. The journey itself can change our definition of success.

We are a culture taught to achieve and accumulate things, but every victory involves struggle and every struggle involves loss. The journey is not always linear or straightforward. Like a butterfly, we can gain strength in the struggle to break free of what is meant to contain us.

What is your dream? If you have never contemplated that question, I encourage you to consider it. Think from the end. What do you hope people will say about you at the end of your life? I believe our biggest fear in life is not death itself but dying without having truly lived. If that is true, how do we fully live as the person we are meant to be? If we strive for success, we may or may not achieve significance; however, if we strive for a life of significance, we will achieve success.

LONGING TO BE REAL

Our dreams are one thing that may push us forward and inspire us to become. The other side of that is our longing for authenticity. *The Velveteen Rabbit* is my favourite book of all time. Although I didn't read it as a child, when this book finally did come into my life in my twenties, it seemed to span time. As much as it transported me to a simpler time in childhood, it also catapulted me forward into questions like—Who will I become? How will I become *real*? It is a story about a stuffed, toy rabbit given to a little boy on Christmas morning. In the beginning, the boy does not pay a lot of attention to the rabbit, which gives the little bunny some time to make a friend and be reflective. The rabbit seems to know about this thing called *real* and contemplates what it would be like to be a real rabbit.

The Velveteen Rabbit is a character just like us—full of hopes and dreams. Yet, he experiences uncertainty and fear about the process. He longs to become real, but he struggles. It is not an easy road, just like life. The principles in the book are simple to understand but putting them into practice is not always easy. In her book, *The Velveteen Principles*, Margo Raiten-D'Antonio helps us put the principles of the children's book into practice. She seems to understand what the author of the original story, Margery Williams, was trying to portray.

The principles are our guide. Perhaps even a talisman—something to anchor us to the truth. *Becoming* is the most important thing we can do in our lifetime. Our consumption-based world boils everything in life down to some purchase that's meant to make us happy. Shame is the by-product if we do not obtain this dictated life. Being busy keeps us in bondage to this object-focused world. How often do we stop to challenge what we've been taught? Or have chased after that job, promotion, or relationship only to have it ring hollow in our lives? We long for meaningful connections to our self, others, and the world. We can only do that once we have become real.

Our longing to be real shows us as silently screaming—physical ailments (pain, dis-ease), emotional distress (anxiety, depression). This can happen when we are more in relationship to things than to the people around us. Isolation and loneliness often precede longings to experience something real. The Velveteen Rabbit is quite certain there is actually such a thing as real. He had only heard of real rabbits after all. He is also afraid that the process of becoming real will be painful and scary. Yet, in the times when he has solitude, all he can think about is his dream of becoming real. We may be the same. Have you ever fixed your eyes on something and longed for it so badly that you ached? Even though the process of getting there is uncertain, there are markers that indicate you're on track.

The Velveteen Principles outlines what the process of *becoming real* looks like. These are principles that can be incorporated into daily life. Real is one thing; becoming is another. All we can do is be active participants in the process and trust that it will lead us where we long to go.

Living from a Place of Compassion

Empathy and compassion for ourselves and others is the first step in becoming real. It is something we must believe. It comes from deep within. Even if there is no evidence that we can become real, there is a longing we feel compelled to follow. It takes time, dedication, and is fueled by love. We follow the same path the rabbit did in the story of *The Velveteen Rabbit*. A path that includes exploration, courage, and time to figure out how real feels to us. We are social and need relationships to help us feel safe and secure. It is up to each of us to discover our talents and share them with the world. It's scary, and perhaps risky, but it is also incredibly rewarding.

As young children, we are taught to push down our feelings. It may become difficult for us to recognize feelings in ourselves or other people. **Empathy is real**. It is about connecting to something in ourselves to make a meaningful connection with someone else. Unless we process our feelings, they do not go away. Interacting with the difficult parts of our story (our grief, loss, trauma) can be tough, however.

Risking is Part of Being Real

Bravery in the face of mockery and the risk of rejection helped the little rabbit on his journey to becoming a real rabbit. He was not brave when he began, nor was he real. Bravery grew out of his desire to become real, even though he may not have seen this bravery in himself. If our goal is to be real and live with purpose, then our imperfections become less shameful. We are broken, flawed, imperfect—and that is okay when we are real.

Once we know who we are, we share it with others and the world. We are generous with ourselves. All of us have gifts and they grow when we give them away. Appreciating the value in everything around us begins with awareness. You become genuinely appreciative of the everyday. Sunshine or rain, you can be grateful for both.

Being grateful is an action—Something you DO

Think about the language we use to describe gratitude. We hear a lot about the importance of being grateful. Some people find time each day to think about the things in their life for which they are grateful. Some use gratitude journals, others use prayer. Gratitude is a description of your current state or attitude. It's a way of showing that you're thankful. Now, what if we switched it around? What if, instead of *being grateful*, you are a *grateful being*? A grateful being is a description of who you are. It's not an action you're taking, a specific way you're feeling, or a display of your gratitude. It's your essence.

In terms of mindfulness, you would be in a constant state of gratitude. Every encounter or interaction would be experienced with gratitude as your frame of reference. As a grateful being, you would notice the little things. For example, imagine you are soaking in the bath after a long week. You would not have to think about things you are grateful for; it would be part of the experience—the hot water, in your home, washing your hair, enjoying a few minutes to yourself.

As a grateful being, you live authentically. You are not just looking on the bright side or trying to find things to be thankful for in the sea of awful things happening in the world. Gratitude is your worldview by choice; and cultivation is key. Contemplation and reflection bring you into a state of gratitude and moulds you into a grateful being. Consider the following:

- What got you through difficult times in your life?

- What lessons did those experiences teach you?

- What is the lesson or meaning for which I am grateful?

- How do difficult times shape my character?

We have become a society of people who love to share their stories of trauma as a way of feeling connected. All of us have struggles and we share our experiences as a way of normalizing them. "I am not alone" is what social movements are all about. That said, if we simply share the story without any reflection, we cannot produce any change. Sharing may actually make us feel worse. The purpose of talking about a traumatic event is to be heard and validated. It is also to learn and grow. My favourite part of the Velveteen Rabbit's story is a conversation between the Skin Horse and the Velveteen Rabbit on becoming real. "Does it hurt?" the Rabbit asks the Skin Horse. "Sometimes," they reply. Yet, even when we know it can hurt, the pain of being *unReal* is more significant. Like the little rabbit, our desire to change is so great we take a chance.

Being Real Means Being Flexible

Flexibility helps us respond to problems in a creative way. Inflexibility is why the mechanical toys in *The Velveteen Rabbit* break so easily. They are afraid to change so they're stuck maintaining the status quo. Real involves exploration, discovery and curiosity. These things allow people to be themselves, without pretense.

First, we need to have self-empathy. Then, we need to extend that empathy to the world in a way that promotes human equality. If your heart is longing, it may be the pull from your own childlike innocence and your desire to be real—whole, connected to something bigger, yet somehow simple. Follow your heart. It can open up a whole new world.

FINDING YOUR WHY

"Life is difficult."

I read that over 25 years ago in M. Scott Peck's book *The Road Less Traveled*. Many people today say they cannot find their passion. Their enthusiasm for life is gone and they feel as if they are just going through the motions. Life seems meaningless at times, which is why each day feels like a struggle. The truth is that much of life is a slog. Our ancestors spent their days walking around looking for their next meal and that was pretty much it. We spend our days running around to meetings, dragging our kids to clubs or practice, managing a million things at one time. It can be easy to lose a sense of purpose in the chaos. The difference between those who feel stuck and those who are content is the difference between those who see routine as meaningless and those who are in love with the process of living.

Discontent can happen if we don't have a why.

- Why did I marry this guy again?

- Why did I want children?

- Why did I leave my secure job to become an entrepreneur?

- Why did I take on so much debt?

Around the 18-mile mark of a marathon is where you'll end up wondering if you've lost your mind—so understanding your why is vital because life is the longest marathon you'll participate in. Why keeps you in the race. Why keeps you moving forward when you feel like giving up.

On a particular stretch of my own marathon, my marriage was struggling, hard. Grief over our losses threatened to take over and destroy our relationship. Day-to-day, we could not imagine getting through the fog, so we went back to the beginning. Why did we get married in the first place? For us, it had to do with the values we shared and the goals we had for our future. These things were bigger than our current struggles. Focusing on our shared values pulled us out of that deep dark hole. It took a long time but our values kept us grounded and hopeful. Their light helped us navigate our way back to one another. We find a partner because we value commitment. We have children or pets because we value family. We go to school because we value education or we choose not to go because we value independent learning. We paint or play music because we value creative expression.

Passion fuels meaning in life. People say they cannot *find* their passion. The truth is that your passion is not lost and you do not need to look for it. However, you may need to *discover* it deep inside you. You need to dig deep so it can be uncovered and then shared. Digging for your passion and purpose involves questioning. Take one of your core values and ask yourself, "What is it about this value that is important to me?" Whatever the answer is, keep going. "What is it about *that* that is important to me?" There is no right answer. You are just exploring. You will know when you find the answer you need—usually several layers down. Trust the process and don't let your brain distract you with overthinking.

Purpose is about finding out who you are and then sharing it passionately with the world. "What you do is less important than *why* you do it and for whom", says Simon Sinek in *Start With Why*. You can recognize the opportunities and the people that show up to help you fulfill your purpose when you know what you truly value. You can instantly see the connection and how it fits in. Once you connect to it, you are free. Free to give yourself fully to everything you do. You do not do it for any other reason other than feeding your soul. It is an expression of you. It is why you are here.

Do you feel as if you are constantly trying to make sense of the world? Things never seem to settle down. A couple of years before I wrote this book, I lost three high school friends in a single year. The first died from cancer. His death brought me face-to-face with my own mortality and made everything I want to achieve feel more urgent. And, due to the sudden nature of his death, it caused me to take stock of my life. "Is this the life I am meant to be living?"

When we live governed predominantly by the rational mind, we are constantly looking to make sense of our world. Have you ever had a difficult or unexpected encounter and then have that story continue to loop over and over in your mind? It's your brain trying to put the events into a logical sequence. Because we are dominated by reason, our brain works hard to rationalize events that seem random. It is safer when things are predictable. A traumatic event can make us feel unsafe. It puts this feeling that the world is unpredictable square in our face. Our response is often to make sense of it in a way that shows how things logically played out. The problem comes when we try to answer big life questions exclusively with our rational brains.

We are surrounded by messages that often hold us back from living fully who we are meant to be. These voices are those of society, the masses. They tell us what to think, how to act, who to be. They tell us how to feel about ourselves and set unobtainable standards. It can often hold us back from discovering our authentic self or from pursuing our purpose. It puts us in a box so that we hold together a system that is not necessarily in our best interest.

Our survival depends on our ability to question. To push, change, adapt—survival of the fittest, and all that. Honestly, I want my life to be about pondering questions and seeking answers. Asking and seeking are just as important as finding the answers. In fact, we will never have all the answers. But then, there is no final exam in life. It is the process of asking questions and seeking knowledge that leads us to truth. And the truth is: I don't know what the meaning of life is sometimes. (Keepin' it real.) We all have moments when we feel lost.

To find meaning in your life, regardless of circumstances, is a key part of the process. It is what keeps us moving forward. It is the search to make sense of the world. In the movie *City Slickers*, the main character, played by Billy Crystal, gets time alone with the old cowboy, Jack Palance. He takes advantage of the opportunity and asks question after question looking for wisdom on the meaning of life. The cowboy shakes his head at all the worry and asks, "Do you want to know what the secret of life is?" Then, he holds up his finger and says, "One thing." As Crystal's character ponders what that one thing might be, it hits him: **the one thing is different for everyone**.

Our "one thing" is the reason we do anything. It is us playing out our purpose or intention in life. It is up to each one of us to find that one thing. We cannot sit around and think about our purpose, we need to go digging for it and seeking it out. Sometimes that one thing is right in front of us, like it was for Crystal's character. All it requires us to do is lean in a little more to who we are; hone our individual skills and talents, and then share them with the world. Our purpose requires us to keep showing up day after day as active participants in our life story.

The truth is that none of us really knows for sure why we are here. Our job is to discover it. It doesn't mean we can't enjoy the ride in the meantime. Spend time watching a sunset, or walking on the beach, or patting your dog. Those things are a meaningful part of the process. They rejuvenate us and keep us going. Remember toward the end of the movie *Wizard of Oz* when Glenda tells Dorothy she had the power to return to Kansas whenever she wanted? The problem was Dorothy. She had not built up belief in herself. She had to discover her power. Our stories are like hers. We find ourselves in the middle of a storm. We are lost and then we become determined to follow the path that leads to the answer. Along the way, we meet a host of characters. There are challenges because the journey is meant to strengthen us and teach us something about ourselves and one another. That we have the power within us to discover that one thing that keeps moving us forward.

In both movies, the characters learn the lesson at the end. We can only imagine what comes next. They return to their everyday lives, but as new people, forever changed by the journey itself. *The Hero's Journey* Joseph Campbell talks about in his work. Finding meaning and purpose in life is possible if you take stock, find your gifts, and choose to be yourself, unabatedly. You are writing your life story, living your life on purpose and with intention. The details will sort themselves out as you go.

MY STORY

Losing my children—Finding my purpose

It started with Sam. I saw him on the ultrasound when he was 18 weeks old. He had full, beautiful lips and big feet, just like his dad. It was the first time in my pregnancy I felt good. I had been so sick with this baby—Pneumonia, extreme fatigue, and mental numbness top the list. Some days I could barely remember my own name. Then I saw that tiny little hand waving to me from the ultrasound and I knew it was worth it. Getting ready for Christmas Eve dinner, I had a different feeling. It was a coldness that seemed to begin from somewhere deep within. It permeated all the way through me. I thought it was the flu. A few weeks later, I knew differently. "We cannot find a heartbeat," the doctor told us at our next scheduled appointment. How could that be? I just saw him. He was fine.

The next 24-hours were a whirlwind of too many choices—delivery, naming, holding, funeral, cremation. This was the hospital's way of ensuring all women have the same options, but their timing felt careless. Left to my sorrow after delivering Sam, I felt the arms of God wrap around me. God's tears mixing with my own. I kept thinking about the line in the Bible that says, "Jesus wept." Even though in that story, He knew the ending.

Lazarus was going to be raised from the dead. Just because Jesus knew the ending did not mean He was without sorrow. I do not believe things happen for a reason. Things just happen. I believe that God holds us gently in times of struggle. As gently as I held my baby in my arms. For me, it was a lesson of Grace. At that moment, I felt that healing was possible.

When I found out I was pregnant again, and that the due date would be exactly a year after losing Sam, it felt like fate. The second pregnancy was better—not as tired, no sickness. It was not until 12-weeks that I even started to get nervous. As I crept closer to the 20-week mark, my nervousness increased, but my dreams kept reassuring me that everything would be fine. My 18-week ultrasound showed the baby was small for her gestational age so I was put on bed rest to help her grow. Late into the second week, as I laid down for a nap, I felt that familiar cold feeling spreading and I just knew. When my husband came home from work, I told him that our baby had died that day. My suspicions were confirmed four days later at my doctor's appointment when I insisted they check for a heartbeat before doing anything else. Silence. A full week after I knew she had died, I was admitted to the hospital for delivery. Later that night, I had Tess, my only girl. This time, I wept with confusion. I felt sure that everything would be fine. How could I have been so wrong? I had taken away such a powerful lesson the first time. I was consumed with why. *Why was this happening again?*

In the months that followed, my sadness was profound. I was so sad that I physically ached. My chest felt hollow. I felt alone, abandoned by everyone—even God. My husband was angry. It was his way of dealing with another loss. I felt completely lost. Where was the lesson? It took many months before I recognized it. It was a lesson of Faith. I needed to keep walking, alone, through the darkness. I needed to trust that the light would come, even if I could not see a glimmer. For a long time, I was uncertain whether or not to try again. In the end, I was willing to take the risk. I believed that I would be okay regardless of how the story unfolded—the lesson of faith. Knowing God would hold me gently through any outcome—the lesson of grace. These lessons were powerful for me. They sustained me.

The third time I found out I was pregnant, I took my maternity leave right away. I wanted to spend every single moment cherishing my role as this baby's mother regardless of the outcome. Seeing my baby on ultrasound, I was overwhelmed with love. I was his mother and he needed me to be strong for him, to love him, to sing to him, to be present. I felt incredibly blessed when he turned out to be a really good sport by kicking at regular intervals, letting me know he was ok. Even though the last few weeks of my pregnancy were uncertain, I felt confident he would be born healthy. And he was. He was such a delightful little baby that I used to call him Sweetness.

The first year after he was born, I had to make a conscious (often difficult) choice every day to live in joy even though my heart still grieved for Sam and Tess. The struggle I went through to have him was a lesson in Strength. The recovery phase is where the muscle builds strength. I needed to remind myself of that. I am indeed stronger having gone through these chapters of loss and healing. It has led me to my purpose—counselling and writing about healing and hope. Now, when I meet a woman who shares her story of losing a child, we share tears. We hold each other gently, knowingly. It is a profound way of connecting to another woman—the mother in me acknowledges the mother in you. For that, I am extremely grateful.

LIVING A "WHAT IF" LIFE

We all long for more time to do the things that bring us joy. Things that align with our values in some way. If we never have time for quiet moments of reflection, life flies by, and we are shocked when it's over. What if, at the end of our life, we realize we forgot to slow down and enjoy it? Even the difficult things in life can add value. We have created a world where managing day-to-day is difficult, and then we judge ourselves for caving under pressure rather than questioning the system itself. Routine can help us manage a busy schedule, but it can take on a life of its own. It may begin to control us instead of the other way around.

What if I live to be 102? Statistically, the earlier you retire, the sooner you die. If I want to live to be 102, it means I can never really retire. What if I can have a life I love now? What would that look like? Would I need to retire at all? We arrive to our various institutions each day (daycare, school, work) and then rush home so we can continue our scheduled lives (practice, games, clubs.) Our behaviour perpetuates a system many of us would not have chosen. When we cannot cope with "normal life", we medicate or implement coping strategies: a short-term fix to get us back to being productive citizens. There does not seem to be any value in just *being* human. I realize we all have bills to pay, but we seem to be trading too much of our life's happiness to pay them. Weekends and vacations are often about catching up from a busy week and doing the things we have neglected, like chores. Sometimes we can sneak in some fun or rest. We get glimpses of fun and harmony and contentment. We go away and spend time at the beach or on a lake. It is enough time to give us an itch. "Now, THIS is the life." But, it is not enough to pull us into serious contemplation.

We may feel we are disadvantaging our children if we do not give them every opportunity. We want them to have every advantage to compete in the world. Yet every hour spent on a team or studying is one less hour of just doing nothing but being a kid. It could be an opportunity to learn that just *being* rather than *doing* is the key to happiness. What if we said no to this harried way of life? It is one of the reasons people may die when they retire. They are worn out and cannot recover enough to enjoy their life. They do not know or have forgotten what brings them joy. We only get one life, and most of it is spent pursuing things that are *supposed* to make us happy rather than things that *actually* bring us joy. That's why people get what they think they should have to be happy, and then they are not happy.

When I ask people what truly brings them joy, it is usually time spent with family or friends. It is helping someone in some capacity. It is curling up with a good book. It is not the fancy life we are taught to aspire to. What if doing yoga every morning brings more contentment than a second car? Can you make that work? Once I realized that I would probably work in some capacity my whole life, I asked myself if it were possible to have that life now. I am taking a chance on yes! I love the work I do as a therapist and can imagine doing it throughout the second half of my life. What if I only had to work part-time? That would give me time to do other things I love like writing, gardening, and travelling. It may mean cutting back in other areas, but the trade-off is worth it. I can picture myself living for another 50 years with that life.

What does your "what if" life look like? What if you can craft a life you would love to live to the end? What if that life could start now? These questions open up a world of possibilities for your future. The healing work we do can open up space for new ideas of how we want to be in the world. It is not about surviving circumstances in life or even endlessly striving to set and meet goals. It is about setting up your life so that you thrive each day doing everything you can to experience all that life has to offer while leaving your mark on the world.

REFLECTIVE ACTIVITY
Let's Get DREAMING

Take the activities we have done so far – the Life Graph, Life Dimensions, insights from your Free Writing or Empty Chair exercise. Drawing on these new perspectives and understandings, ask yourself this question:

If time and money were no object, what would I do with my time? What would I do with my life?

Spend time exploring and dreaming. If you find yourself caught up in how you would do it, bring yourself back to dreaming. There are no barriers.

You may want to take this activity a step further and do a vision board. Look through magazines and see which pictures you are drawn to and cut them out. I noticed recently that all the pictures on my dream board had water. Apparently, I am a water person. Who knew? This is another exercise in discovery.

Life is about discovery as much as it is about creation.

CHAPTER NINE

SETTING YOUR *Intention*

How to take the next step in your life journey

"Infuse your life with action. Don't wait for it to happen.
Make it happen. Make your own future.
Make your own hope. Make your own love."

Bradley Whitford

"Some people dream of success, while other people get up
every morning and make it happen."

Wayne Huizenga

Our world has become so hurried that any amount of slowing down feels as if we are falling behind. It seems we all race against this invisible clock. We have no time to be still. Clients come to see me at 20, 30, 40, even 60 years of age, saying they feel behind. Their lives are not what they expected at this particular age. "What did you expect it to look like?" I ask curiously. Most often, they are unsure where they should be, but know it's not where they are at that moment.

Typically, we measure progress based on acquisitions—partner, children, house, career. That is what time is: a measurement. It is arguably a social construct since the US standard for time has only been around since 1883. It came with the railroads and the need to schedule production. Work weeks are in days. In some countries, you work five days, in others six. Weekends only exist in relation to the workweek. In agricultural communities, time exists in seasons. There are seasons for planting and those for harvesting. You harvest when the crop is ready. It seems time is fluid rather than fixed when you think about it that way.

One of the most confusing statements around grief is that time heals all wounds. If you think about it from the point of view of a physical injury, time is a factor in healing. My friend had open-heart surgery and there was an expectation that time would be part of the healing process. There is no timeline in grieving. It is more like the seasons—days seem to be getting warmer, and then it snows. Some years are cold and rainy others are warm and dry. Each season is unique. Grief is like that too. One year is not better than another simply because it is further away from the moment grief began. To measure it against standard time is not helpful. The time following a significant loss can feel foggy. You forget what day it is. Everything slows down. Nothing seems to make sense. You may feel you're going through the motions and time is an illusion.

Emotional injuries take time to heal, just like physical ones. All healing takes time, but you have to be sure to "set the bone", so to speak. If you do that, time may indeed help. How do you do that on an emotional injury? Emotional healing is not as simple as "look on the bright side" and other such toxic positivity. In fact, I think that kind of advice is hurtful, and potentially harmful. It is more about taking the time to examine where you are—the extent of the injury. My friend's surgery took 6-hours in the operating room, but it took months to heal fully.

Healing a broken heart after a loss is no different. *Convalescing* is an old term, it used to be a large part of the recovery process. It comes from the Latin "to grow fully strong". Convalescing includes fresh air, sunshine, exercise, healthy foods, and rest. It was seen as necessary to have time away from everyday pressures. Day-to-day life now feels terribly complex. When our system is overwhelmed, the simplest thing takes us off course, from making dinner and doing housework to going to an appointment. It can leave us feeling ridiculous for being unable to cope with basic tasks. Living in a stressful state can take all the strength a person has for the day just getting out of bed in the morning.

Depression is often our soul's way of retaliating against the prescription of busy. It has a way of protecting us. Feeling depressed is our fundamental need for *deep rest*. Our society wants to quiet that voice with antidepressants, as if being in a state of depression is to be avoided at all costs. For anyone prone to clinically depressive episodes, additional emotional injury may require medication. That does not replace the need for rest. Resting is the best medicine for healing, yet we never seem to consider convalescing a necessary component anymore.

Our brain needs to make sense of our circumstances, which is why we replay stories over and over in our head. Like depression, it may feel uncomfortable. As if something is wrong if you cannot seem to stop the thought loop. Taking the time to allow our brain to catch up with what has happened is part of the process. If life sucker-punched you, and you are now flat on your back, why not lay there for a little while? Take a moment to catch your breath rather than rushing back to being busy. Take time to contemplate what's next.

I know this is not possible in every situation. Everyone's life is different, and we may not have the luxury of taking time for healing. You may have to return to everyday life before feeling ready. You may need to cut back on other demands so you have time to breathe. Unplug where you can. Rest. It starts with permitting yourself just to be where you are. Carve out time to convalesce, whatever that looks like for you, and regain your strength so you can properly heal. Allow life to unfold on your time. Most things will wait for you.

LESSONS FROM THE TORTOISE

If you want to do something different or meaningful, it means dedicating yourself to something beyond what is typically prescribed as success. Everything in our social world today points to hustle, like in the story of *The Tortoise & the Hare*. Many of us are like the Hare. We take off strong but then get distracted by every new and shiny thing that comes along. Success is a long game, yet the media emphasizes overnight success.

Everything needs to be quicker, stronger, faster. Most importantly NOW! The Tortoise in the story brings us key messages we can expand upon. Lessons such as:

Start!

Tortoise knew he did not have the same advantages as Hare, but he did not criticize himself for his lack of skill. He also knew he did not have the same connections or upbringing, so he did not focus his attention on it. He just started walking. Other lessons from the story were simple too:

Show up every day!

Tortoise dedicated himself to the race. Although he knew he was unlikely to win, he committed to finishing. That made all the difference in how he handled the race. He decided to show up and do a little more each day. Eventually, he would finish. Most importantly, he competed only with himself.

Learn and adjust!

The tortoise did not know what the whole track looked like when he started. He could only see a certain distance in front of him. Some days, he could not see the path at all. He adjusted as he went. Some days were better and he went further. Some days were difficult and he barely went more than a few steps. As the terrain changed so did he.

Never give up!

Finishing was the goal. Tortoise soon forgot about Hare altogether and just focused on what he could control—his own journey. He did not fight with himself daily about whether or not he should be in the race. He just set his intention on finishing and never thought about it again.

The moral of that story is that once you decide to run the race, go all in. It can feel overwhelming doing something different from the rest of the world. There is lots of chatter from society on what path we should be travelling. Choosing to run the race at all is a risk. You don't have to know everything before you begin. Just get started, then learn and adjust each day. As dedicated as you may be to your race, others may think you're nuts. You are out there committed day-in and day-out. Whether starting a business, working on your relationships, healing from your past wounds, stay the course. You may not cross the finish line tomorrow but keep showing up in your life.

LIFE CYCLES

There is a time for everything. What season are you in now? We will all be born. We will all die. Society today sees life as linear. We talk about the journey, which indicates you start in one place and walk until you finish the path. We are expected to hit milestones along the way. Typically, we hit them in a predictable sequence: we are born, go to school, graduate college, get a job, get married, buy a house, have children. When the kids grow up, we do everything in reverse. Personally, I know very few people for whom this story is true. Myself included. Many of us do things out of order. We backtrack. Get stuck. Some of us will die well before all these expectations are accomplished. At the end of the race, as at the end of life, people regret more the things they did not do than the things they did. Even if they get pulled out before the race was completed, they can be proud that they ran the race at all.

The Life Graph you did gives you an overview of your life. You can make it as colourful as you like by adding pictures or emotions. The point is that by linearly looking at our lives, it may be easier to catch the themes and patterns that show up repeatedly. It can also be helpful to give perspective on why an event was so significant. For example, if you lost a parent at a young age, you may also have moved and switched schools. Eventually, you may have had a step-parent with new siblings. Losses tend to come in clusters.

Looking back at my Life Graph, I can see that January is the most common month for me to make radical life decisions. It inevitably follows a season of stress. A time when I want to run away and live in a cave. Just for a while. I would find myself leaving school or jobs. Looking at your life across time organizes your story into chapters so you can course correct.

Along the way, we have to continue to ask questions to make sure we are not drifting aimlessly away from the things we've deemed important in our lives.

- Where are you now?

- How did you get here?

- Where do you want to go?

- What does your story tell you?

- Can you identify cycles in your life?
  (Perhaps 7- or 9- year patterns.)

It may be helpful to look back through your story from time to time looking for things you learned about life and about yourself. If we shared our Life Graphs with one another, I bet we'd find that our cycles look similar. We have all had difficulties. We have all had triumphs.

CULTIVATING HOPE

It seems we are at a very pivotal point in our world's journey. What can I do as an individual in a world such as this? It can leave us feeling hopeless. I am only one voice. But, so are you. It seems impossible to change the world as an individual. However, working collectively for a common purpose can shift the trajectory of the planet. It is called the Butterfly Effect—one small shift can make a big difference. I believe that shift begins with hope. Hope can grow from crisis, which is where things seem to be now in our world. Crisis allows us to open up to new and creative possibilities. I've heard it said that the story begins after the trauma. If that is the case, then the story can be one of hope and healing. Cultivating begins by understanding the following:

Hope is a Mindset

Hope pulls on elements of positive psychology, a scientific field of study focusing on positive human functioning in all dimensions of life—biological, personal, relational, institutional, cultural, global. Hope is not a personality trait. It is not something we are born with necessarily. Hope is something we cultivate and hone in ourselves and our lives. It is about well-being, quality of life, contentment, and meaning in life. There can be meaning in suffering if we look for it.

Suffering is an ineradicable part of life, but just like all things in life, it can be meaningful. Our world is suffering but I believe that when things happen (good and bad), they can be a springboard for change. There is a reason we secure our own mask first when the air pressure drops in the cabin of an aircraft. Heal yourself, then heal the world. Hope has been proven to be the key to patients healing themselves from illness and disease. If that is true for individuals healing the self, then why not heal the world through hopeful people in action.

Hope is Agency

Hope is the feeling of control over our lives and our world. It is our belief in our self and our ability to set goals and imagine multiple pathways to reaching them. We all get to choose how we look at our past. We all have baggage. Your experiences can make you or break you. They ultimately change who you are in the world, but the good news is you get to decide how. Resilience is about bouncing back. Traumatic growth is about taking the opportunity to reflect on who you are, what's important, and how to make a difference in the world because of what you have learned. That growth can be transformative. If you have gotten back up from a traumatic experience, you have built your resilience muscles. You have the strength to get up again. Keep building your strength. Keep getting up. Keep transforming. Keep becoming. We are the hope for future generations. We must lead from a place of strength.

Hope is an Action Word

We can make the world a better place by making small meaningful changes over time. It starts with each of us individually. Everything we do on a small scale has a big impact when enough people are engaged in the same behaviour. We can do a little bit each day to influence our path forward. We have overwhelming national debt; aim to live debt-free. We see violence and aggression around the world; be kind. Bullying has become an epidemic; be a friend. When the rest of the world is silent; write letters, march, protest. As the world seems to be self-absorbed; serve.

Times of crisis and tragedy were the times when Mr. Rogers' mother suggested he focus on the helpers and on the good still happening in the world. When there is tragedy and despair, be a helper. Although it may seem small and insignificant being only one person, cultural anthropologist Margaret Mead encourages us, "Never doubt that a small group of thoughtful, committed citizens can change the world; indeed, it's the only thing that ever has."

Hope is Risky

Remember the Sesame Street character Lefty? He was the guy with the trench coat and black fedora who always tried to sell you something you need, like air. He once convinced Ernie he needed air to breathe, blow up a balloon, and play his harmonica. All true. Ernie took a risk. Lefty got a nickel; Ernie got a handful of air. When I started my blog, I decided to call it *Peddling Hope*. That was risky. Peddling is a word that has become synonymous with promoting unorthodox views. In a world of war and despair, hope may be just that—a contrary and perhaps radical way of seeing the world. But, risks lead us places and stretch us. If you want success, you need risk. If you want innovation, you need risk. If you want longevity, you need to be taking risks that other people may think are too risky, ironically.

Hope is Foundational

Hope is more than a desire or a wish. It is an intention and expectation for the future. It is a philosophy by which you live your life. It is a fundamental belief that we can make a positive and meaningful impact in the world regardless of our present circumstances. That's what I say on my website anyway. Taking a risk on the word "peddling" is a way of standing up for what I believe in. Hope exists like air. You cannot see it but that does not mean it does not exist. I would argue we need hope just like we need air. How else do we shift the planet's trajectory towards a brighter future for our great-grandchildren? Hope means taking a risk today for someone in the future.

EVALUATING RISK

We hear all the time that risks are necessary for business. That does not mean you take uncalculated risks. *Inc.* magazine contributor Minda Zetlin wrote a piece called 5 *Things the Smartest Leaders Know About Risk-Taking* that talked about risk. That risks should align with a company's mission. If you are considering a personal risk, do you have a personal mission statement for your life? Companies that have mission statements may be more willing to take risks in order to fulfill their mission. A personal mission can work in the same way. How do you know if the risk will bring you closer to your aspirations if you are unclear on what those are? The students I work with often struggle with taking risks. "Should I try this course? What if I fail?" They can become paralyzed with fear. If the objective is to obtain a well-rounded education, the risk may be worth the reward. Think about what can be gained—necessary skills, new information, and the knowledge that you can take risks and succeed. Alternatively, it may teach you how to fail. That is the nature of risk. Failing is part of success.

Zetlin says there are two more things to consider beyond aligning with the mission statement. Risks come with costs, and you have to be okay with failure and loss. She also says it is okay *not* to take a risk. That is where the calculated risk comes in. Is it worth the risk to go for it? As long as the answer is based on something other than fear of failing, the answer is maybe *no*. Remember, the rewards of taking risks are not necessarily immediate, which means it can be challenging to see how a risky decision pays out until long after the decision has been made and executed.

How do we make these calculated risk-taking decisions? Basic things to consider when making a decision or evaluating risk are:

- Do you have enough information (or maybe too much)?

- Have you consulted anyone else (or perhaps too many)?

- Did you consider people's vested interests in either changing or staying the same?

Most importantly, did you consider the emotional attachment aspect? Change involves loss. And, even though it may be worth it for the risk, it can still be difficult to move in a different direction.

My great-grandmother was a risk-taker. She moved from a small town in Newfoundland, Canada, to the large city of Boston in the United States when she was just 15-years old. She went to help her cousin through the birth of her first child, and she stayed for several years after she met my great grandfather. They eventually settled in Nova Scotia, where he had three children from a previous marriage that ended when his wife died died in childbirth. Three months after her 9th child was born, my great-grandmother lost her husband to cancer. The oldest of the nine children, just 14- and 15-years old at the time, got jobs to help her manage the farm. They helped her move to the city, buy a house, and raise the children.

The stories of my Grammy were always of her strength—childhood diseases, the Great Depression, two World Wars—I cannot imagine. She died when I was 10, but I craved stories about her struggles and the risks she took. I am sure my great-grandmother thought about the consequences of every choice she made. Ultimately though, she led with her heart. What would be best for her family? She was a woman of character and great love. She was a pillar of hope for the future. Like her, I believe that risks are often worth taking in an effort to align with our mission in life.

WHICH WAY DO I GO?

You go where you look. That is one of the things they teach you when learning to drive a car. It is the same in life. Knowing where you are going is important because that is where you will end up. We are in perpetual motion and do not have much time to stop and think about our destination. Even when we have some idea, how many times in life have we come to a fork in the road and have no idea which way to go?

When Alice in Wonderland came to a fork in the road, she asked the Cheshire Cat for guidance. He asked her first, "Where do you want to go?" Alice responded that she did not know, to which the Cat replied, "Then it doesn't matter." Maybe we had a plan but now we feel unsure. The fork in the road is an opportunity to re-evaluate our destination. Or, it is a chance to be more precise about where we are going. A chance to determine if the road we are travelling is getting us where we want to go in life.

Forward View

The landscape around the fork may be nice, so you decide to settle there. Sometimes settling down is in your best interest. Often, we do it only because everyone else seems to have settled down. We follow the crowd. How often do we take the time to make sure this place is where we are meant to be? If it is, great! Settle in. If not, keep going! The fear of making a mistake by picking one road over another may be paralyzing. Quiet contemplation is part of the process of determining the best route.

Rear-view Mirror

It can be helpful to glance in the rear-view mirror from time to time. Seeing how far you have come may give you the confidence and strength to go on. You can see how much you have overcome and how capable you are on the journey. The challenge is that you cannot drive forward if you constantly look backward. One of the more beneficial uses of the rear-view mirror is identifying blind spots. These may be the assumptions and biases you have collected over the years. It can be very helpful to consider where you want to go based on where you have been. You may decide to travel a different road. A road that will take you to places you have never been before. The point is to check your rear-view from time-to-time to inform the journey, but looking backwards too long can be dangerous long-term.

Side View (or "Rubbernecking")

Have you ever been stuck in traffic, knowing there is an accident ahead, then finding no road obstruction at all? The drivers have simply slowed down to check things out. Rubbernecking to see what is happening around them. That happens in life too. Our journey can be slowed by paying too much attention to what others are doing. Focusing too much on the drivers around you can stunt your journey. Rubbernecking in life sounds like: Where are they going? How'd they get that shiny, new car? Are they pulling ahead of me?! Perhaps it sounds more like: Where is everyone? Are they on a different (faster, better, healthier, wealthier) road than I am? How do I know where to go?

James' Story

James was a client who came to see me saying he felt stuck since his wife died. He kept going around and around but was not getting anywhere. He wanted to get off what felt like a perpetual merry-go-round but had no idea how to do that. There were several exits off the track. James had to look at where each road may lead before deciding. He and his wife had always dreamed of retiring to their cottage and travelling. James was only 60 and felt it was too early for that road. With a little time to think things through, James had an idea. What if he planned a trip to coincide with his retirement? He and his wife had talked about Europe. James wanted to do an adventure tour while his wife dreamed of small towns where she could have coffee each morning and watch the people move about with their day.

As James talked through this idea, he started to feel his enthusiasm for life return. The plan to hike the Camino Trail began to take hold. He would have his adventure, but each morning would stop for coffee to spend a little bit of time holding the memories of his wife. Although he lost her too early, he felt incredibly grateful for the life they built together. Sometimes the only way to move forward is first to slow down.

If you are uncertain about your destination, slow down so you can work through all the possibilities. If you are worried about making a mistake, you can always double back and make a different decision. Slow down long enough to check in with your heart. Focus on yourself. It can be such a distraction watching what everyone else is doing. What do you want to do? Take one step in that direction and see how it feels.

When you come to a fork in the road, use it to your advantage. It is a chance to slow down, regroup, recharge, refuel. It is a chance to check your map. Are you on track? Check your mirrors. See how far you've come. Life is a crazy journey sometimes. As you move through it, don't forget to slow down long enough to enjoy the ride.

ANATOMY OF A HABIT

Did you know that it takes 18-254 days to develop a new habit? Many people think it is 21 days, but in a study published in the *European Journal of Social Psychology*, Dr. Phillippa Lally studied habits and found the average was 66 days. That's over two months! In a consumer society, we're conditioned to expect results instantly. We see something we like, we buy it. When we decide to do something different, we expect things to change right away. Because we decided, we expect the results to follow.

Habits take a little longer. They need time to form. I heard a statistic recently that said only 14% of people who make resolutions stick to them. That seems incredibly low. The study noted that 66% of people who make resolutions give up at two months. Based on the previous study, people give up before the habit is fully formed. It makes sense that if we expect our habits to be in place within 3-weeks and it still seems to be a struggle at that point, we would give up. New habits follow a pattern and take more than willpower to maintain.

Anchoring habits in your values helps you find a fundamental reason for the change. But understanding the process may help too. It is more complex than the typical "cue, behaviour, reward framework" you may have read about. Habits are patterns. They can be helpful (watching a show at the end of the day to unwind) or harmful (binge-watching to avoid social situations). Your behaviours and patterns will be different from someone else's. Even if you have similar resolutions, your ability to keep up with them will vary. The first step to understanding the anatomy of your habits is observation. Rather than thinking about the new habit you are trying to institute, think about the old habit you are trying to break. See if you can identify the loop.

Marcia's Story

Marcia vowed to give up junk food in the new year. To ensure her long-term success, she needs to understand what reward she gets from it. Thinking back to the times of day she would reach for unhealthy snacks, Marcia identified the feeling of frustration. Treats had been part of her upbringing, something special to make her feel better. Our interactions with other people predominantly centre around food at holidays, celebrations, or even getting together with friends after work. Marcia had come to identify treats with comfort. As she reached for these particular foods, her thoughts turned to "I deserve it." After a long day, or at the end of a frustrating interaction, Marcia felt she deserved a reward for getting through it. In the moment, she identified feeling soothed, calm, relaxed. Later, those feelings would turn to disappointment in herself for eating unhealthily and annoyance at her weak will. She would fall into a "what's the point" slump and feel uninspired to make a change. She could quickly identify the basics in the loop when I asked:

- **Trigger Thought**: I had a hard day.

- **Behaviour**: Eat a bag of chips watching TV.

- **Reward**: Feel soothed in the moment.

Really what she was looking for was the reward of feeling soothed. Most articles you read on forming new habits will stop there. The general feeling is that if you can identify the payoff and then replace it so you still get the reward, then you can change the habit.

New habits often lead to new anxieties. Take away the bag of chips, and you take away the soothing feeling, which can leave you feeling anxious. One of the challenges that many people do not anticipate is the stress that comes with change. The other is that often the habits we want to change are caught up in emotions. Marcia would need to deal with the frustrations using strategies other than eating, if she wanted to stick to her resolution. Simply dealing with the stress of change, new habits can be formed using a problem-focused approach.

Neural pathways in the brain are like roads that help to transport information from one area to another. Imagine a habit being like a route you take from point A to point B. Your neurons know the way. Doing something new means learning the new route and then giving it time to be as well-worn as the path before. It is your brain relearning. It is possible to forge a new pathway; it just takes repetition. It helps when other positive reinforcements are available. Things that make you feel good for taking the new (and perhaps uncomfortable, unfamiliar) route. That enables the habit to stick.

Habits closely connected to emotions require an emotion-focused approach to break and replace them. To break her habit, Marcia had to learn to speak up for herself to avoid feeling frustrated. That was a little more challenging than simply changing her eating patterns. Regardless of whether they are problem-focused or emotion-focused, expect a little bit of stress to come with new habits you are trying to form. Make getting through those barriers and obstacles part of the process. If you fail, know that it takes time to train your brain. Think about or document what happened and see if you can find a solution to deal with it the next time it happens.

THE GIFT OF SELF-MASTERY

Action is only the first step in developing a new habit. It is the time when you learn what works, and how to work through setbacks, before making modifications and adjustments. Once the habit is set, maintenance can carry you forward. The new habit becomes a part of your identity. It does not mean old patterns are gone forever, but they may be easier to identify and overcome. "How's that working for you?" I joke with my friends and family when they come to me for free therapy. They get the hardcore, tough love, Dr. Phil-style therapy from me. When we are trying to break a habit or make a meaningful change, something inevitably holds us back. This question is a good place to start. The truth is we do things because they work.

My client Brittney longed to be in a relationship but just could not seem to find one. I suggested that maybe it would be easier to find one if she actually *looked* for one. If she wanted a relationship, she would have to risk being vulnerable, and that scared the hell out of her. Even though she said she wanted a partner, staying single was safe. Staying single was working for her on that level. Her fear of risking being vulnerable was more significant than her desire to meet someone. Seeing how the patterns were working at keeping her stuck was the first step in changing her story. When we consider a change in our life, we have to get clear on what we need to do and how to do it. The most important question to answer is *why*. Why do I want to change?

Stages of change can help emotions that seem stuck in complacency move forward. Understanding the stages tackles the how; as in, this is how you move through the stages to make meaningful, long-term change. Awareness that you have something you want to change is the *what*.

- What do I want to change?

- What do I do to change it?

Why we want to change connects to our values and aligns us with our personal mission statement. Self-mastery is about getting to why. I believe much of the reason we feel unsafe in our society today is that there is little stability in our lives. Children will push the boundaries and then retreat when they find the limits. That is why consistent discipline is important in raising kids. Both my kids would get sick if they ate too much junk food so I'd limit it. Why? I'm expected to take care of them. The same is true for all of us, although I cannot always apply the same expectation with myself when there is Party Mix involved.

Maslow says we have two competing forces—one towards growth and one towards safety. We set boundaries because we love our kids. We want them to be safe. When they know you are in control, they can relax and have fun. They have healthy attachments and are much less anxious as adults. Many of us have grown up in unstable households with abuse or addiction. Quality time wasn't invented until the '80s, so many adults grew up with a lot of independence (or neglect). Perhaps setting boundaries for ourselves, perhaps not. If that is your story, setting boundaries and expectations will feel foreign and may be difficult to maintain yet they are key elements of self-mastery. The child in you will want to push the boundaries to see if they are real, not wishy-washy.

The biggest hurdle to your discipline is the part of you that is a rebellious teenager. Adolescents tend to push back, wanting to do everything themselves, without limits or controls. Tough love requires being very firm with that part of our self. Otherwise, the teenager will be at risk for a lifetime of poor choices. The thing is, we have to figure this out on some level. Maslow contends that, "If you deliberately plan to be less than you are capable of being, then I warn you that you'll be deeply unhappy for the rest of your life. You will be evading your own capacities, your own possibilities." That is pretty hardcore truth. Yet, he's right.

Often, the reason people have for being unhappy is that they did not think life would turn out like this. Brittney thought she'd be happily married by this age. She's an amazing person who has the ability to be in a loving relationship. The longer she stays stuck in her fear, the more miserable she becomes. There is a ton of stuff out there on the art of self-mastery. The key is to remember that it is a practice—a set of daily habits that you can depend upon. When the world goes sideways and your legs get swept out from under you, the habits you have established for yourself can help you feel safe.

COMPONENTS OF SELF-MASTERY

Belief

The single biggest thing you need to conquer is your belief that change is possible. Once you have established that, you need to make some progress quickly. Do one thing to shift the story. Of course, you will be fighting your instinct towards homeostasis—the desire to move things back to the state of equilibrium you have established in your life, no matter how unhealthy it is for you.

Belonging

Once you believe you can make a shift, it is key to surround yourself with people who will support your growth in that direction. It can be in-person, like joining a support group, or it may be finding a group online. Perhaps people who are trying to make the same changes you are. While they may say they support your decision to change, friends and family may sabotage your progress. Frequently, it is unconscious. They desire to maintain the status quo to stay safe.

Behaviour

Although belief and belonging are key, things move a lot more quickly when we move to the action stage. If you are ready (awareness) and have a plan, start! You do not have to get good and then start. You have to start and *then* get good. It will not feel natural at first, and you will need to set up your life for success. Do one thing. It will shift the focus from thinking to doing. All things completed daily are called a *practice*. That is what we do. We practice. It is in practice itself where self-mastery is achieved. These are the everyday practices that keep us in a natural state of good health. Our system knows how to thrive by healing and repairing. Daily habits, rituals, and routines keep our emotional system ready to support us through challenges and change.

In his book *Reinventing the Body, Resurrecting the Soul*, Deepak Chopra says, "The rhythms of the body need to be healthy because they are the most basic way that you keep your life properly timed—every cell synchronized with every other. The more irregular your lifestyle, the harder it is for this delicate, complex coordination to exist." Life is a glorious dance. All we need to do is learn the steps and keep moving.

REFLECTIVE ACTIVITY

Visualization – Inner Adviser

As you relax in your favourite spot, close your eyes and bring yourself into a state of relaxation. Allow your inner wisdom to come into your vision. Imagine what this adviser looks like. What are they wearing? Are they tall or small? Perhaps they are not a person at all. Your inner adviser might be an animal or some other creature, or simply a colour. Imagine your inner adviser now.

Your inner adviser reflects your inner life, a wisdom that has been passed down through the ages. Some call it intuition or ancestors. Tell your adviser you will not push for simple answers to important questions. Let your adviser know that you would like to establish an ongoing dialogue so you can connect periodically for advice.

If there is a problem that has been bothering you for a while, ask your adviser if they are willing to give you help with it. You can ask your adviser anything at all. Simply use your breath. Bring your attention to your breath now.

- Pose your question, then as you inhale – ask.

- As you exhale, hear the first response that comes into your mind.

- That is your inner adviser's reply. It may come in words or an image.

- Continue with your dialogue for a few moments, asking any other question that is on your mind. Inhale, ask. Exhale, receive the answer.

Remember, your adviser is wise and knows everything about you, but sometimes, for a very good reason, is unable or unwilling to answer your questions. This is usually to protect you from information you may not be ready to hear or deal with. If your adviser does not answer a question you ask, ask instead what you need to do in order to make this information available to you. Your adviser will usually show you the way.

One way your adviser can help motivate you to continue on your journey of self-mastery and growth is by giving you a clear picture of the benefits you will gain. Ask your adviser to show you what your life will look like next year, in 5 or 10 years.

- Is there anything you would like to tell your adviser? If so, do it now.

- Is there any final question you would like to ask? If so, do it now.

- Is there anything your adviser wants you to reflect upon? If so, ask your adviser to bring that into your awareness now.

- Thank your adviser for meeting with you today. Let them know you are looking forward to meeting again soon.

AFTERWORD

I recently saw a series of pictures of the moon taken at the same time each day for one year, then collated into one photograph. The various phases of the moon, taken over time then presented together, formed the symbol of infinity. Think about that for a moment. The moon's cycles follow a pattern each day, each month, and the overall result of that pattern is a symbol of infinity. In western society, we see time as linear. We think about our life as having a beginning (birth) and an ending (death). Really, according to the moon, it's infinite—endless, boundless.

As I prepared to write this book, I reviewed personal journals that I have kept since I was 25 years old. They represent snapshots of my life. Like the moon, I found patterns that were cyclical rather than linear. Looking back, I have cycled through a similar storyline—discontentment, struggle, reflection, and growth. No specific ending or beginning. Each phase lasting for a stretch of time. Each time seeming to learn (or relearn) whatever I needed to understand in that moment to move on. Then, I would inevitably cycle back through each phase again.

If I had the written words in a visual form, they would also show a pattern. When I think about it visually, I imagine my life's journey as a sphere. I am the object rotating through a pattern as it spirals towards my authentic self. Of course, the authentic self is not the perfect self. Perfection is not attainable. Human beings are not perfect, so constantly reaching outwards to pursue the *perfect self* leads to frustration and feelings of worthlessness. Reaching inward to connect with the *authentic self* is different.

Just as Michelangelo says he simply chipped away the excess marble to find David contained within, we can find our authentic self in the same way. We need to remove the barriers in our environment that threaten to take us off track from finding and living our purpose. We cannot do that by living only in survival mode—that state of anxiety and threat. Rather, we need to focus on setting goals and intentions that we strive towards and learn to thrive in that process. Great, how do we do that?

SURVIVING

The basis of evolutionary biology is survival. Darwin took it one step further in his theory to say that it is *survival-of-the-fittest*. He postulated that only those who could adapt to the often-dangerous world would survive while everyone else perished. If we consider that idea through the lens of evolutionary psychology, it means our thoughts, feelings, and behaviours are all directly linked to staying alive to influence the next generation. Not only that, but evolutionary psychology means everything we encounter in daily life is a potential threat to our very existence, which is really helpful in dangerous situations but not as helpful otherwise.

When there is uncertainty in the world, our system filters everything as dangerous so that our core neural system (the amygdala) prepares the body for threats. It increases blood flow, tenses the muscles, reduces digestion, and narrows our range of focus. Animals react this way when they are in danger of being eaten. Humans, however, react that same way, but not always in response to a life and death threat. More often, it is the presence of abstract rather than direct stress that fires up our nervous system; for instance, paying bills, public speaking, relationships, or a new environment can create that same bodily reaction as a threat to our life.

Learning to live mindfully in the world one day at a time is the only way to pace the stress and not overwhelm the nervous system. **Satipatthana** is a type of mindfulness that is based on paying attention—sati (attention), pa (inside), tthana (to keep). *Keep your attention inside.* Observing our thoughts and feelings rather than reacting to them is key. It begins by observing our reactions with curiosity, our wise mind. This approach to mindfulness is a way to settle our nervous system. It grounds us in the present moment and reminds us we are safe. We do that by incorporating basic activities into our daily life.

According to a study at the University of Ottawa called *How to Stimulate your Vagus Nerve for Better Mental Health*, they tell us that 'Vagus' means 'wanderer' in Latin, as this nerve looks as if it is wandering all over the body, and it is the core of our ability to survive. We can achieve optimal health of the Vagus nerve with:

- Cold exposure (showers, ice baths, swimming in low temperatures)
- Deep and slow breathing; Meditation or mindfulness
- Humming, chanting, singing, gurgling (throat vibrations)
- Probiotics (for good gut health) and omega-3
- Exercise; massage; socializing and laughing

How many of those do you make time for in your daily life? Daily practice builds resilience, which is needed to keep our system prepared for inevitable change, rather than continuously scanning our environment for danger or living in a state of stress and overstimulation. Once our Vagus nerve is confident we will survive, it allows us to move on to experiencing the non-threatening parts of the world where we can confidently strive and thrive.

STRIVING

We strive to conquer new feats from the moment we're born—crawling, walking, running; as well as sounds, words, sentences. Unless there is something impeding that growth and development, it unfolds naturally in its own time. Curiosity seems to be part of human nature, pushing us to try new things and helping us adapt to new environments and our newly acquired skills as we go. However, those around us can make this striving to learn and grow a competitive endeavour, which can be destructive. Even the word *striving* itself comes from the Middle English word "strife" meaning "to quarrel or fight". There is a shift from simply exploring and growing as a part of human nature to striving to meet milestones before your peers.

Our environment is set up to be competitive. It can start with parents comparing their child's development against a scholarly source or their friends' kids. We somehow convince ourselves that our child is brighter if they walk a month before the kids next door, which can make new parents feel proud. Schools have a grading system that ranks students against one another, often separating learners in a way that reinforces labels like high- or under-achiever. Scholarships and awards for academics and athletics become the cornerstones of success as a young person. Some would argue that we are training students for the "real world", which, in free-market capitalism, is competitive in its structure. Competition for internships and jobs reinforce the belief that we must be better than our peers to achieve an edge.

Competition is not a bad thing. It can help us stretch ourselves and improve our skills. It can be the motivation needed to set and achieve goals. However, it becomes problematic when we live only from this place of comparison. The ego can become over-developed while our overall sense of self suffers. If we only focus outward and constantly compare ourselves to others, it limits our ability to find our authentic self. Feeling as if we are consistently falling behind or not measuring up can impede our ability to see ourselves as capable. Social media adds a new layer to our desire to do as well as we perceive the highlight posts of the people around us to be their everyday success rather than a snapshot in time. There seems to be this external expectation and pressure to reach some bar that is perpetually out of reach.

Of course, we need to strive for things. Setting goals is a way to bring the life we desire to fruition. But, we also need collaboration to succeed without slipping back into a place of survival as our primary objective. Margaret Mead was a social anthropologist who believed the first sign of a civilized society was a mended bone. In a survival-of-the-fittest scenario, an animal or person with a broken bone would die. A mended bone was evidence of someone caring for the well-being of another at their own risk. "Helping someone else through difficulty is where civilization starts," said Mead.

I believe what Mead's work shows is that we have survived as a species precisely because we have cultivated collaboration and caring for one another rather than merely competing to survive. Focusing on striving to meet only our individual needs means we are not fully thriving in life.

Thriving requires us to cultivate and live in a system of care that focuses on community.

You may wonder, how can we incorporate goal-setting and striving for excellence in a way that leads to a life of thriving? It's all about where you put your attention:

- Focus on mastery or excellence rather than perfection

- Live in the process rather than only thinking about the outcome

- See mistakes as part of the process

- Balance the pursuit of mastering new skills and reaching new heights with self-care and service to those journeying with us

THRIVING

Dr. Daniel Brown, a sport and exercise specialist at the University of Portsmouth, UK reviewed all the existing literature on the topic of thriving to see if he could find the underlying principles we can apply if we want to thrive in our daily lives. He worked alongside Dr. Rachel Arnold, an expert in the psychology of performance excellence, to develop a multi-faceted concept that includes psychological, physical, and social enhancements in life. Their explanation of what it means to thrive in life came down to "an individual experiencing a sense of development, of getting better at something, and succeeding at mastering something. In the simplest terms, what underpins it is feeling good about life and yourself."

What struck me about their work is that the elements of thriving are the intangibles—being motivated, committing to learning and expanding, being resilient and socially competent. These are not things easily measured and they are nearly impossible to compare with others. For instance:

- Thriving is about cultivating a daily practice that grounds you in the present moment.

- Rituals and routines are a crucial part of providing a level of predictability for the nervous system as we ride the rollercoaster through times of chaos and stability in our life.

- We thrive when we find the right daily practices for our goals and lifestyles.

- Hope is a key element of thriving.

In fact, hope is a foundational principle by which to live life. Regardless of our circumstances, we can take what has happened to us and make something meaningful, to understand ourselves or life more fully, and pass that wisdom on to the next generation. Hope is the fuel we need to thrive on our journey. Everything we experience changes the way we view ourselves or the world around us.

I entitled this section of the book an afterword—some last bit of sharing to create enthusiasm for the journey following its reading. But it is really about what comes afterward. In fact, it is all about what comes after. For those who have stuck with the book to the end, the journey continues from here. Healing is a process. It is one of the elements in creating a life where you are thriving in the unpredictability and instability that comes with an ever-changing world. We need to be nimble and adaptable.

As young children, we adapted to survive but as adults we can adapt to thrive. The difference is in our intention. That intention needs to include adapting to change by looking at every situation as an opportunity to grow and learn. Being aware of our environment, as well as our ways of inter-acting with it, is a start. Going back to look at our lives through the lens of healing and hope becomes part of moving forward and living our lives to the fullest. Setbacks should be expected, but knowing what our per-sonal challenges and triggers are can be the difference between moving through those setbacks and growing or getting stuck until we finally learn what we need to learn.

Once we see the world in this way, through a lens of self-awareness and opportunities for meaning and growth, we cannot be any other way in the world. If we choose not to do the work of conquering a challenge, we'll know. There will be a part of you, the part that encouraged you to keep reading, that is dedicated to the process from here. That part will know and provide encouragement. The idea is to continue to move and change and adapt. All the while becoming who you are meant to be in the world—your unique, authentic self.

The world has been here for a very long time. It's a mystery as to why we are here, at this exact moment in time. Yet, here we are. What will we do with the time we have? It's a chance to pull the world in the direction of love and connection. I believe that is our collective purpose—to love one another while we are here and infuse that love into the next generation. Our individual purpose is simply how we, with our unique strengths and talents, fit into the collective. That is how we weave the tapestry, write the story, and paint the masterpiece.

We are each a thread, a chapter, a brush stroke. We come together to tell the story of creation as it unfolds and becomes all that it is meant to become. My hope in writing this book is for you to share with me in the process of becoming. You've become part of this writing in a unique way by engaging with it. I hope to continue writing and that we will continue to walk together for as long as we are all part of this larger creation called humanity.

ACKNOWLEDGEMENTS

The desire to write a book took root as ideas for healing and hope in a blog and in my practice as a therapist took form. The actual writing took longer than anticipated; however, I was never alone as I wrote and the chapters unfolded. All the authors who came before me encouraged the process as I drew on their collective wisdom. I have quoted many of them and encourage the reader to seek out their work.

Thank you to my husband, Dan Bishop. This book could never have happened without your support. Your steadfast love and desire for personal growth makes you the perfect companion on such a journey as walking the road less traveled.

Thank you to my mom who gave me and my siblings the space to explore and be who we were meant to be in the world. It has not always been an easy path for any of us. Yet, "we glory in tribulations knowing that tribulation produces perseverance; and perseverance character; and character, hope." Romans 5:3-5

Special thanks to my Uncle Larry, whose desire for this book to be done so he could be mentioned in the acknowledgements really did keep pushing me forward. Thank you to all my 'fans' who read and shared and commented on my blogs and social media posts. Your encouragement to get things out there, especially when a part of me wanted to retreat into my own solitude, kept me on schedule and producing.

My biggest and most heartfelt thanks goes to Crystal Picard, who guided me through the process of editing and publisher-ready. Your professional experience and honest feedback made the book better than it was before we met; and, your vast experience made launching the book as successful as it could have been. Thank you, infinity.

RECOMMENDED READING

Chödrön, Pema. *Start Where You Are: A Guide to Compassionate Living.* Shambhala Publications. 1994.

Lesser, Elizabeth. *Broken Open: How Difficult Times Can Help Us Grow.* Villard, NY. 2008.

Maté, Gabor. *When the Bod Says NO: The Cost of Hidden Stress.* Knopf, Canada. 2011.

Brown, Brené. *Daring Greatly: How the Courage to be Vulnerable Transforms the Way We Live, Love Parent, and Lead.* Penguin, UK. 2013.

Brenner, Helene. *I Know I'm in There Somewhere: A Woman's Guide to Finding her Inner voice and Living a Life of Authenticity.* Penguin. 2004.

Schwartz, Richard. *No Bad Parts: Healing Trauma and Restoring Wholeness with The Internal Family Systems Model.* Sounds True. 2021.

Learner, Harriet. *The Dance of Anger: A Woman's guide to Changing Patterns of Intimate Relationships.* Harper Collins. 2014.

Peck, M. Scott. *The Road Less Traveled: A New Psychology of Love, Traditional Values, and Spiritual Growth.* Simon & Schuster. 1987.

Solomon, Andrew. *The Noonday Demon: An Atlas of Depression.* Simon & Schuster. 2015.

Wilbur, Ken. *Integral Psychology: Consciousness, Spirit, Psychology, Therapy.* Shambhala Publications Inc. 2000.

James, John W. & Friedman, Russell. *The Grief Recovery Handbook: A Program for Moving Beyond Death, Divorce, and Other Devastating Losses.* Harper Collins. 1998.

Vanzant, Iyanla. *Yesterday I Cried: Celebrating the Lessons of Living and Loving.* Simon & Schuster. 1999.

Van Der Kolk, Bessel. *The Body Keeps the Score: Brain, Mind, and Body in the Healing of Trauma.* Penguin Publishing Group. 2015.

Porges, Stephen W. *The Polyvagal Theory: Neuro-physiological Foundations of Emotions, Attachment, Communication and Self-Regulation.* WW. Norton. 2011.

Dana, Deb. *The Polyvagal Theory in Therapy: Engaging the Rhythm of Regulation.* W. W. Norton. 2018.

Kushner, Robert S. *When Bad Things Happen to Good People.* Anchor Books. 2004.

Seligman, Martin E. P. *Authentic Happiness: Using Positive Psychology to Realize Your Potential for Lasting Fulfillment.* Atria Paperback. 2002.

Siegel, Daniel J. *Mindsight: The New Science of Personal Transformation.* Bantam Books. 2011.

Howard, Alex. *Decode Your fatigue: A Clinically Proven 12-Step Plan to Increase Young energy, Heal Your Body, and Transform Your Life.* Hay House Inc. 2021.

Frankel, Viktor E. *Man's Search for Meaning.* Beacon Press. 1959.

Moore, Thomas. *Care of the Soul: A Guide for Cultivating Depth and Sacredness in Everyday Life.* Harper Perennial. 1992.

Singer, Michael A. *the untethered soul: a journey beyond yourself.* New Harbinger Publications. 2009.

Friedan, Betty. *The Feminine Mystique.* W. W. Norton. 1963.

Ware, Bronnie. *The Top Five Regrets of Dying: A Life Transformed by the Dearly Departing.* Hay House Inc. 2019.

Kegan, Robert. *The Evolving Self: Problem and Process in Human Development.* Harvard University Press. 1982.

Baxter Magolda, Marcia B. *Authoring Your Life: Developing Your Internal Voice to Navigate Life's Challenges.* Stylus Publishing, LLC. 2017.

Mezirow, Jack. *Learning as Transformation: Critical Perspectives on a Theory in Progress.* Wiley. 2000.

Saunders, Matthew L. *Becoming a Learner: Realizing the Opportunity of Education.* Macmillan Learning Curriculum Solutions. 2018.

Williams, Margery. *The Velveteen Rabbit.* Simon & Schuster. 1922.

Raiten-D'Antonio, Margo. *The Velveteen Principles: A Guide to Becoming Real.* Health Communications Inc. 2004.

Sinek, Simon. *Start with Why: How Great Leaders Inspire Everyone to Take Action.* Penguin Publishing. 2009.

Chopra, Deepak. *Reinventing the body, Resurrecting the Soul.* Three Rivers Press, NY. 2009.

RESOURCES

How to Stimulate Your Vagus Nerve for Better Mental Health – www.sass.uottawa.ca